NOSTALGIC STAFFORD

The publishers would like to thank the following companies for their support in the production of this book

Main Sponsor

ALSTOM T&D Limited

Benton Memorials

Davies Motors Recovery Services

Horsleys of Stafford

H Nickolls & Son (Milford)

Perkins Engines Company Limited

Stan Robinson (Stafford) Limited

Stafford Railway Building Society

Dean Statham

Ed Weetman (Haulage & Storage) Limited

First published in Great Britain by True North Books Limited
England HX3 6AE
01422 344944

ISBN 1 903204 64 X

Text, design and origination by True North Books Limited
Printed and bound by The Amadeus Press Limited

Introduction from ALSTOM

Our chapter in this book clearly describes how Stafford has a strong electrical manufacturing history. Throughout it you will read many business names such as English Electric and GEC, but the successors name is ALSTOM and we are proud of our history.

Stafford remains the centre of ALSTOM's UK Transmission & Distribution operations and we have a strong commitment to maintaining and developing our business interests in the town and continuing to be a part of the local community.

ALSTOM today is a world leader in our field; in Transmission & Distribution alone there are over 33,000 employees based at more than 80 industrial sites world-wide. We cover the entire power spectrum for the supply of electrical energy, from generating stations to final consumers.

We are proud of the heritage we have and the Company that has grown from it. Around the world people know that Stafford is the home of Transmission and Distribution solutions; this is not a reputation that has been created overnight. It is a legacy of all those who have worked on our shopfloors, walked our corridors, designed our products and delivered reliable systems.

Our product and service offering is now considerable; we can not only provide equipment to transmit and distribute electricity around the world, we also sell energy management systems which perform billing and metering processes. We now have people who work constantly on maintaining the infrastructure that brings electricity to your home and we even keep the railways running. Transmission & Distribution in the UK now employs more than 3,000 people, has a turnover in excess of £250 million and we regularly export to the four corners of the globe. We have come a long way since the opening of the first Lichfield Road works in 1903, but if it were not for those 100 years we would not be what we are today.

We hope you enjoy reading about our intricate history and that of the town that we are proud to call our home.

Contents

Introduction

The historic town of Stafford, some 27 miles north of Birmingham city centre, 56 miles south of Manchester and 139 miles from London, lies at the very heart of England.

The borough of Stafford covers some 230 square miles and is home to more than 126,000 people. It is also host to almost 4,000 businesses; over the years the name of the borough has become known across the globe through local companies such as GEC Alsthom, Varity Perkins and Unicorn International. In recent years the town has also become renowned for its association with high technology through the Staffordshire Technology Park on the edge of the town, adjacent to the campus of Staffordshire University, home of the Octagon Centre for computing.

But Stafford is not all business and technology. The borough and its immediate environs can boast some of Britain's finest countryside: Stone for example, just eight miles north of Stafford, on the Trent and Mersey Canal, is still a vibrant, bustling market town and waterway centre: once it was also the home of the renowned Joules Ales as well as Hovis bread. And if delightful country towns are not enough to satisfy visitors to the area there are plenty of historic houses and museums to take a peek at.

It's more than a thousand years ago that Stafford gave its name to the surrounding county of Staffordshire. And despite the passage of so many centuries the historic borough is still very much the 'County Town': it remains the centre for local government, business and the law, whilst Stafford's ancient Market Square is still at the heart of the town's busy commercial centre.

The story of Stafford goes back well before the Norman Conquest: in the late 9th century it was Queen Ethelfleda of Mercia, a daughter of Alfred the Great, who first turned Stafford into a fortress to repel Danish invaders; the town which grew up around those defences would be home to a royal mint for 250 years from AD 924.

In the years following William the Conqueror's successful invasion in 1066 the strategic importance of Stafford was

Great Heywood residents celebrating VJ Day in September 1945.

recognised by the Norman invaders. William ordered new defences to be built to provide his followers with protection from a still hostile and rebellious local population. By 1100 the Normans had built a massive timber fortress.

The growing town of Stafford got its charter in 1206, but over the following centuries the fortunes of the castle, and of its keepers, the Stafford family, fluctuated considerably. In 1347, a founder member of the Order of the Garter, Earl Ralph, built a massive stone keep on top of the motte: a century later, in 1444, Humphrey Stafford was created Duke of Buckinghamshire and Stafford castle reached its zenith.

Life though was not all preparation for war: a surviving inventory taken in 1537 shows how herbs were an important part of daily life at the castle. They were widely used for their medicinal, aromatic and edible properties. From that detailed inventory, a new herb garden was recreated in the castle grounds in recent years designed with sixteen beds, each containing herbs related to specific illnesses.

Sadly, in the early 17th century, the castle's fortunes declined. During the early part of the Civil War it had been defended by the Gallant Lady Isabel but it was doomed to be abandoned and demolished along with the town walls. Royalist Stafford had withstood early attacks by Oliver Cromwell but the town eventually fell to the Parliamentary army in May 1643.

Today Stafford's Ancient High House is one of the finest remaining Tudor buildings in England, and the largest remaining timber-framed town house in the country. When it was built it dominated Stafford's skyline. In 1642, the year before the town's surrender to Cromwell's forces, King Charles I stayed at the High House on his way to Shrewsbury. Ironically John Bradshaw, the town's MP, went on to preside at the trial of Charles I and to be a signatory of King Charles' death warrant. Happily, if anachronistically, the castle would be largely rebuilt in the Gothic Revival Style in 1813 before falling into ruin once again in the 20th century.

Today, in the 21st century, and at the beginning of the third millennium, this book is dedicated to all those readers who take unashamed pleasure in nostalgia. This is not however the kind of dry, boring history book which so many of us were made to study in our long-gone school days: instead it is a vivid reminder of our own history.

Here within this book's covers can be found images of 20th century Stafford, from times now just on the edge of living memory, to what may seem like the day before yesterday - until we gasp with astonishment that 20 years or more have inexplicably elapsed since we last looked on a scene depicted here.

This carefully chosen collection of photographs, with

Gaolgate pictured in 1961.

their memory-jogging text, will bring smiles of happiness, and perhaps some tears too, with their evocations of life in Stafford in the middle decades of what is now 'the last century'.

Are you old enough to remember the war years? Can you recall sitting at home in 1939 listening to Mr Chamberlain's announcement that Herr Hitler had declined to withdraw from Poland and that as a consequence we were at war with Germany for a second time, after just 21 years of peace?

Or are you a little younger: do you perhaps recall the young Queen Elizabeth's coronation in 1953 and the excitement of street parties to celebrate the event? Maybe you are old enough to have experienced the electrifying thrill of hearing rock and roll music for the first time in the mid 1950s and joining in the worldwide acclaim for that astonishingly gifted young man Elvis Presley.

Readers who are younger still will find their memories jogged with pictures of the swinging sixties. Who amongst those who lived through those years can ever forget the Beatles, the Rolling Stones, mini skirts, the arrival of Radio One, colour television and, gloriously capping the decade, that historic landing on the Moon by American astronauts? Is it really now more than 30 years ago that Neil Armstrong said those famous words 'That's one small step for man, one giant leap for mankind'? Was it really as far back as 1979 that Margaret Thatcher became Prime Minister? Goodness how the years fly by. But though world-changing events and internationally famous faces may be important it is the everyday lives of ordinary folk which ultimately matter most. And it is personal memories of life in Stafford which will inevitably be jogged most vigorously by the contents of this book: our schooldays, our first job; the happiness of a first stolen kiss on the back row of the cinema juxtaposed with the inevitable sadness of recollecting names and faces long gone. So go and make yourself a nice cup of tea and plump up the cushions of your favourite armchair. Gather your friends and family around you and delve deep into not only the history of Stafford but your own history too. There's nothing wrong with nostalgia, especially today when even folk well on their way to middle age can no longer recall that 75p once meant fifteen shillings! Yes, history can mean events of a thousand years ago, but in truth history began yesterday. So sit back and enjoy this unique book about our Stafford, a Stafford which still continues to exist in our memories and be cherished in all our hearts.

Street scenes

Below: The four-dial clock seen here in Gaol Square and telling us that it's five past three sometime in the early 1930s, had originally been presented to the town in 1916 by a grateful George Bruckshaw to celebrate his fifty happy years of residence in Stafford. When it had first appeared in the town the fine clock had replaced a third lamp which once crowned the Sidney Fountain (erected in 1889 by the widow of Thomas Sidney, the Stafford man who became Lord Mayor of London, 1853-1854). The third lamp was itself a replacement for a statue of Hercules which had originally crowned the well-loved fountain which, as well as providing refreshment for humans, had featured water basins for both horses and dogs. The drinking fountain was destroyed in May 1928 when a motor van ran into it; though both the fountain and the clock were completely wrecked the clock was later restored and mounted on a new post near to its original site. Behind the clock, on the north side of the Square, is the Singer Sewing Centre, which later became Birches' Radio and Vision Service. Next door but one, the premises occupied by The Jap Co, at 13 Gaol Square, subsequently became F T Parkes, house furnishers. The small shop in-between, with no name emblazoned on its blind, was, back in those days, a sweet shop named the Mecca. Behind The Jap Co Ltd can just be made out the gable end of the old Grammar School building on North Walls.

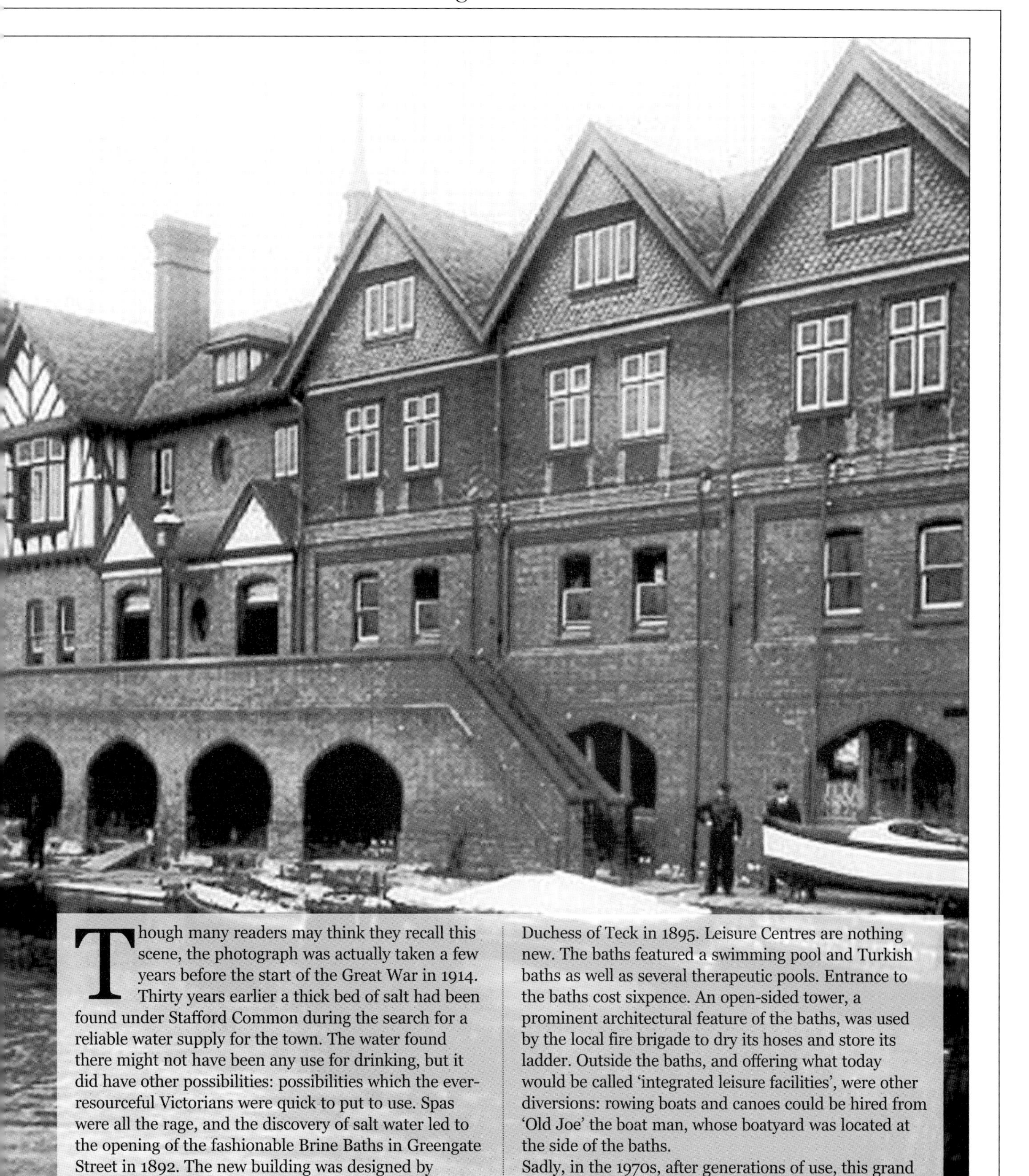

Though many readers may think they recall this scene, the photograph was actually taken a few years before the start of the Great War in 1914. Thirty years earlier a thick bed of salt had been found under Stafford Common during the search for a reliable water supply for the town. The water found there might not have been any use for drinking, but it did have other possibilities: possibilities which the ever-resourceful Victorians were quick to put to use. Spas were all the rage, and the discovery of salt water led to the opening of the fashionable Brine Baths in Greengate Street in 1892. The new building was designed by George Wormald. Its grander title, The Royal Brine Baths, came about as result of a visit to Stafford by the Duchess of Teck in 1895. Leisure Centres are nothing new. The baths featured a swimming pool and Turkish baths as well as several therapeutic pools. Entrance to the baths cost sixpence. An open-sided tower, a prominent architectural feature of the baths, was used by the local fire brigade to dry its hoses and store its ladder. Outside the baths, and offering what today would be called 'integrated leisure facilities', were other diversions: rowing boats and canoes could be hired from 'Old Joe' the boat man, whose boatyard was located at the side of the baths.

Sadly, in the 1970s, after generations of use, this grand building was found to be unsafe, and in 1977 the baths were demolished.

Below: This anything but tranquil view of Doxey Road taken from just over the Broad Eye Bridge during the terrible floods of March 1947. On the left of the scene are the houses which would much later become the local Conservative Party Headquarters. In the background can be seen the flat-roofed Castle Tavern pub whilst over to the right are the railway goods and coal yard.
The scouring action of the water would cause considerable damage to the roadbed not to mention undermining walls and affecting cables under the road. A number of telegraph poles in the town were rendered unsafe. Despite there being far fewer telephones in 1946 than today paradoxically there were far more telegraph poles. Overhead wires rather than underground cables were still the distribution system of choice and poles with multiple lines attached, such as that featured in the centre of this picture, would remain a common site for many years to come.
At the time many people blamed the terrible weather on American and British experiments with atomic bombs. In August 1945 the first nuclear bomb had been used against the Japanese, leading to their unconditional surrender soon afterwards. The surrender had not however stopped more atomic bombs from being exploded. Experimental nuclear explosions had continued at the Pacific Bikini Atoll through the summer of 1946. At the time it seemed quite possible that that there was some direct connection between the awesome power of the atom being unleashed and the appalling weather nature unleashed on Britain.

Peter Rogers

No, this isn't Venice but the centre of Stafford. It's an easy mistake to make when the striped pole bearing traffic directions in the foreground looks more like something a gondolier might moor his boat to. Understandably there's not much traffic about on Bridge Street on this day in 1947. A prolonged period of wet weather resulted in the River Sow rising to its highest ever recorded level. To begin with Wellington boots and gabardine raincoats were enough to keep pedestrians dry, but before long even they were not sufficient. Sensible folk stayed at home if they possibly could. The floodwaters soon reached the railway station and stopped all traffic. At the junction of Newport Road and Bridge Street the water rose until it was thigh deep. Many locals were briefly trapped in their homes and cottage dwellers had to be rescued by boat. Despite a great deal of minor damage and flooded cellars however only one house was completely washed away. Other parts of the country were even less lucky and a number of tragic deaths were reported. In the centre of this tranquil photo is the Grapes Hotel a pub whose regulars would have to risk getting wet outside if they wanted to get wet inside. On the left of the picture is the old library building, a civic amenity which occupied the same site until 1999, when it was moved to part of the Shire Hall on Market Square. The old library building would subsequently be used as an arts centre.

Peter Rogers

In 1953 Stafford's Market Square was laid out with flowerbeds, trees and seating to commemorate Queen Elizabeth II's coronation. This photograph was taken in 1957, by which time locals had got used to their 'new look' Market Square. The timber-framed building next to Boots was Averil's Old Shop. Dating from 1475, the Old Shop had been a chemist's since 1786: it was demolished in 1961. Today it is almost unimaginable that such vandalism in the name of 'progress' could take place. The gardens were a popular feature of the town and added a splash of colour in a world recovering from the years of austerity which followed the ending of the second world war. Those who had been holding their breaths expecting a repeat of the economic misery which had been the aftermath of the first world war were beginning to feel that this time around things would be different - and that the future might hold prosperity rather than poverty. For the few months before this picture was taken however there had been a serious blip in that happy vision. Petrol rationing had been re-imposed in the wake of Britain and France's abortive invasion of Egypt to secure the Suez Canal. From December 1956 until May 1957 petrol rationing would be a reminder that we weren't quite out of the woods yet. In 1992, almost 40 years after the gardens were planted the square was paved and the bus shelter removed as part of the pedestrianisation of the town centre.

BARCLAYS
Timothy Whites & Taylors
Timothy Whites & Taylors
A. DOBSON LTD
BARCLAYS BA

This view along Bridge Street, taken from the roof of the library building, shows street decorations for Her Majesty Queen Elizabeth II's coronation in 1953. On the right can be seen the tower of the Royal Brine Baths.
It was the beginning of a new Elizabethan Age, or so we were told. Part of that new age was television; sales of television sets boomed in advance of the coronation ceremony, the first in British history to be seen live not by mere thousands but by millions.
Those who could not afford a TV crowded into neighbour's homes to watch the BBC's grainy black and white broadcast and to witness the Archbishop of Canterbury place the crown on the young Queen's head followed by the sight of a proud Prime Minster, Winston Churchill, swear fealty to the beautiful new monarch. Twenty-five years after the coronation, on 7th June 1977, we celebrated the Queen's Silver Jubilee. 'Long Live the Queen' reads the banner strung across the highway in 1953, and it was a sentiment that was equally true in 2002 when we found ourselves celebrating the 50th Golden anniversary of Her Majesty's accession to the throne. Now, half a century on from when this photograph was taken, it's sobering to look back and see just how few motor vehicle are about: one lorry and one car in the foreground compared to five bicycles. These days there must be a hundred motor vehicles on our roads for every bike.

HE QUEEN
F H BURGESS
BRITISH ROAD SERVICES

J E C Peters

Above: For more than 80 years Stafford's Mount Street was dominated by the rectory which features in this photograph taken in 1962.
What had by then become the 'Old Rectory' had been built in 1880 as a home for the parish's Church of England rector. The rectory was a notable feature of Stafford until it was demolished in the 1960s; the site would subsequently be occupied by the Iceland store and the Sheridan Shopping Centre.
What may surprise younger readers is just how many cars appear in the picture. Harry Potter fans will immediately recognise the light coloured Ford Anglia almost disappearing at the bottom of the picture, but other makes are harder to identify: how's your memory? Is the van on the left with the sliding doors a Commer or a Bedford 8cwt? One thing is clear - by 1962 Henry Ford's famous adage 'customers can have their cars in any colour they want - so long as it's black' had become part of a past we were all glad to see the back of. The 'swinging sixties' were just beginning and dusty old rectories and black-painted cars held little interest in the extraordinary wave of optimism and youth oriented culture which was about to be launched.
With the glamorous John F Kennedy still President of the US and Telstar the first communication satellite, recently launched, not even the Cuban Missile Crisis and, nearer home, the Profumo scandal 'starring' Mandy Rice Davies and Christine Keeler could stop the tide of progress.

Above right: Though for many readers the early 1970s still seem like only yesterday it comes as a shock to realise that more than 30 years have passed since this photograph

was taken on Bridge Street. Everything here looks the epitome of tranquillity, but that was far from the truth, at least in the world outside Stafford: in Uganda the madman Idi Amin was busy expelling 40,000 British Asians. Nearer home 1972 was a year in many ways better forgotten with strikes by miners, dockers and power workers. Cuts to electricity supplies were the order of the day and would soon become a regular feature of life. The economy was in a bad way too with inflation already around 12 per cent and destined to soar to double that figure.

Taking up the centre of the scene are the premises of Frederick H Burgess Agricultural and Horticultural Engineers whose 'modern' shop sign over the entrance to its store stands in sharp contrast to the original signage at the roofline. Passing by this well known shop, and giving away the fact that the picture was taken many years ago, are the vehicles on the road: on the left is an example of that stalwart of the British motor industry, a Morris van, the commercial version of England's well-loved answer to the Volkswagen Beetle. On the right, just appearing in the picture, is the front of a motor cycle with its number plate lethally placed over the front mud guard ready to slice into some unlucky pedestrian - undoubtedly some things have changed for the better!

This building, in Gaolgate Street, housing Radio Rentals, was the birthplace of Thomas Sidney in 1805. Thomas became Lord Mayor of London in 1853-1854 and in 1889 his widow erected a fountain in his memory in Gaol Square.Thomas Sidney was however a long forgotten figure by the time this photograph came to be taken in 1962.

Though by the early 1960s radios may have been cheap enough for them to be bought outright it was still commonplace to rent a television rather than to buy one. Seven and sixpence (40p) a week reducing to five shillings (25p) a week was a typical price. And that was a fair bit of money back then, but still good value when it included servicing. These days we take the reliability of electrical goods for granted, but those old black and white sets didn't half seem to burn out their valves quickly. Today we've become used to seeing the picture on our screens instantly; not so in 1962. 'Is it on?' was a regular question posed soon after the switch had been pressed. How many of us recall getting up to peer hopefully in the back of the box and see the orange glow from the valves slowly heating up before they would deign to deliver the picture we were all waiting for? And what programmes we watched: there was the still new Coronation Street. Who could have ever imagined then that this gritty northern soap opera would outlive the wireless' Mrs Dale's Diary?

J E C Peters

Below: Here's a scene, which has changed dramatically since it was captured on film in 1962.
Centre of the scene is the Lamb Inn on Broad Eye, which was eventually destined to become a wine bar. How many mature readers can recall enjoying a pint at the Lamb? Today the cost of beer is counted in pounds not pence, but back in the early 1960s, before inflation had taken its heavy toll, a pint still cost less than two shillings, or 10p in today's devalued money.
The single car parked outside the inn is another reminder of just how much times have changed. Even the road surface itself with its complete absence of yellow lines, is itself silent testimony to the happy carefree days of motoring when anyone with a car could drive anywhere and park easily outside the shop of one's choice without being bothered by parking wardens and parking tickets. Looming behind the pub can be seen the huge gasometer of the Chell Road gas works. And hands up if you recall that gas in those days was made from coal, not pumped out of the North Sea!
Over on the left we can just see St Bertelin's Chapel which had been built to replace St Augustine's chapel: consecrated in 1900 it suffered from only having a small congregation and had been closed in 1920. Though the building was subsequently used as a Sunday School it was finally demolished in 1964 at around the same time as the nearby houses.

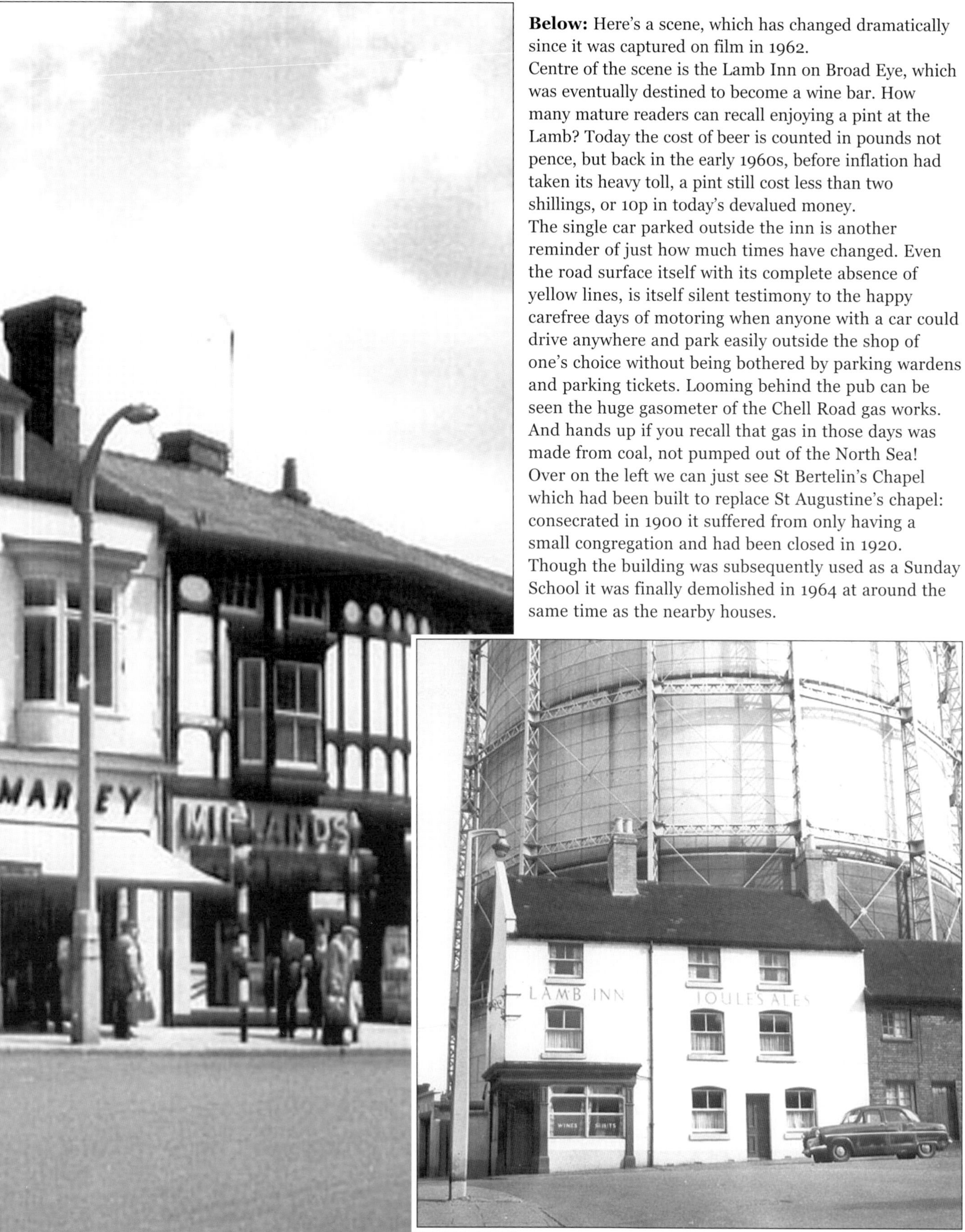

J E C Peters

Below: 'A land fit for heroes' was a slogan that went back to the first world war. For those who returned from the muddy trenches of Flanders or the oppressive heat of Mesopotamia that dream failed to come true. Britain in the hungry thirties with its mass unemployment was not a land for heroes. Having been duped once the country was in no mood for a repetition in 1945. Even so the results of the khaki election of that year came as a shock. On 8th May the war with Germany ended. On 26th July Britain went to the polls and to the amazement of the world Churchill, who had led the country through its darkest days, was ousted in favour of the Labour Party led by the unknown Clement Attlee. This time the workers would not be cheated: the Labour Party really did intend to deliver a land fit for heroes. And that included decent homes. Before the nation's bomb damaged cities could be rebuilt however temporary houses needed to be built. And quickly. The best way to erect new buildings rapidly was to prefabricate them in factories then simply throw them up on prepared concrete bases. In this way thousands of 'pre-fabs' soon sprang up all across the country. This photograph features Exeter Street in Stafford. The scene was captured in 1947 with the road surface still to be laid. Little did those returning heroes know just how long these 'temporary' houses would have to remain in use.

Right: Here we are in the year 1961 looking along Salter Street from Gaolgate. The building on the right, with its ornate facade, was once the Empire Hotel. On the right are the premises of Thorn and Co ironmongers and builders merchants. In 1961 the huge out of town DIY superstores were still something for the far off future. Indeed DIY was nowhere near so popular as it would become. Despite lower incomes folk were still far more likely to get a tradesman in to tackle jobs like painting and decorating than today. Mind you, in those days before non-drip paint, and when wallpaper had to have its edges removed before it could be used, that was probably a wise choice.
As for ironmongery? Well these were still the days before metrication. The back of school textbooks still talked about 'French' centimetres and no one talked about kilograms. 'A pound of six inch nails sir?' Certainly, and none of that metric rubbish! It's ironic that having soundly drubbed the French at Waterloo in 1815, and supposedly consigned their revolutionary metric system to the history books, they still managed to have their revenge.
Though engineering was the first industry to metricate you wouldn't have known it here at Thorn's. Screw threads had first been standardised in England by Stockport born inventor and engineer Sir Joseph Whitworth in the 19th century; he had given us standard 'Imperial' or' Whitworth' gauges for nuts and bolts: you knew where you were with a sixteenth of an inch.

J E C Peters

OWS
ESTIMATES FREE

Events & occasions

No one now living will recall this exact scene. The photograph, thought to have been taken in 1902, shows Sanger's Circus, parading along Gaolgate Street towards Market Square. Though no-one may be around to recall this day in the second year of the reign of Edward VII older Stafford residents may well recall such sights in their youth. And even those not so old may have faint memories of something similar: but watch out, is your memory playing tricks? Maybe what you think you remember was actually watching Circus Boy on television in the late 1950s or early 1960s; a 'period piece' set in the USA and featuring child actor Micky Dolenz, who later found fame as a member of the Monkees, in the starring role.

But if some memories are deceptive others are very real. Yes the Big Top really did come to Stafford and it did so in style. Over the last few decades however the size of circuses has declined and the acts less dramatic, not least due to the activities of animal welfare groups. The number of animal acts began to fall away rapidly from the 1970s, but in earlier years there was no question what one could expect to see at the circus which was never complete without elephants and lions. At least clowns have never changed: most of us found the clowns funny but there was always at least one tot who was even more terrified of them than a whole cage full of tigers.

The 'Baby Day' parade pictured here in Greengate Street in 1928 was organised by the Maternity and Child Welfare Committee of Stafford Council. Prizes were given for the best-decorated prams and for the bonniest baby: judging took place in Victoria Park after the parade. Maternity and child welfare services would remain part of the local authority's responsibly long after the creation of the NHS in 1948. Not until 1974 would all health services be collected together under the umbrella of the NHS authorities. In 1928 such services need all the help they could get, not just from ratepayers but from charitable contributions too. Having a Baby Day was an ideal way to draw attention to the importance of taking care of future generations, though at the time this photo was taken it would be many years before free orange juice, school milk and cod liver oil were standard fare provided by the state to growing youngsters.
Meanwhile back in 1928 this parade of perambulators reminds us how such 'vehicles' have changed down the years. In the days when walking was the usual means of transport prams were everywhere, and old ones were much coveted by small boys desperate to find a set of wheels to make a racing cart.
No new mother felt complete without a Silver Cross pram built like a battleship and capable of carrying not just a baby but a toddler on top and the week's shopping below. Today's collapsible kiddie carriers just can't compete.

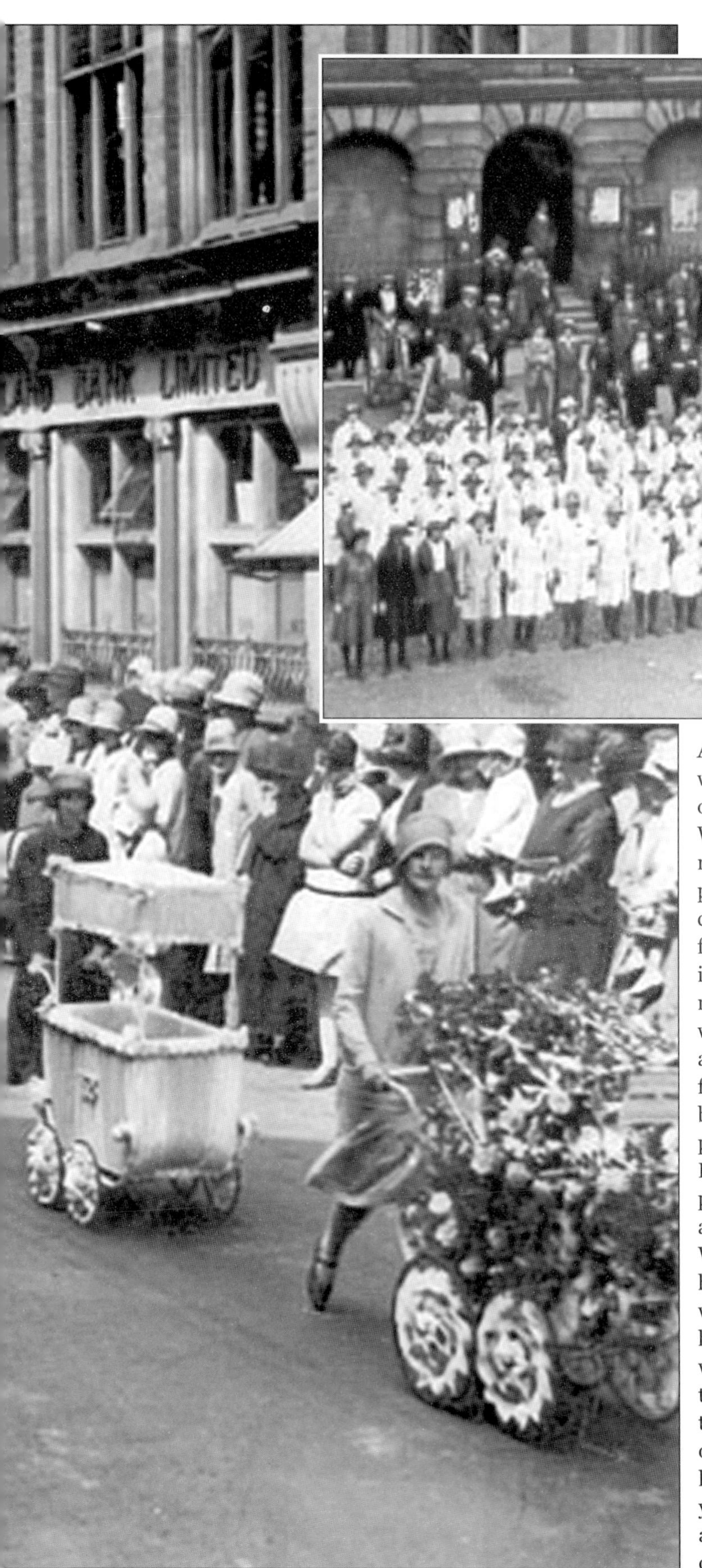

Above: It's 1919, the year after the end of the first world war, known until 1939, with sadly misplaced optimism as the 'Great War' or the 'War to End All Wars'. The scene is Stafford's Market Square where members of the Women's Land Army are on parade. The WLA had been founded during the course of the recently ended war to help combat food shortages: the volunteers filled the vacancies in the agriculture industry caused by the millions of men who had joined the armed forces. During the war years many WLA parades and rallies were held all across the country. Local dignitaries and notable figures attended to make the inevitable morale-boosting speeches as well as to be presented with proficiency certificates and badges.

Here in Stafford members of the WLA are being presented with good service badges by Lady Gaunt and by Mrs Levett, the Chairwoman of the Women's War Agricultural Committee. The women lined up here in serried ranks had much to be proud of: without their sterling efforts many in Britain would have gone hungry during the dreadful four years when so many men were away fighting and dying in the trenches of northern France. No doubt in 1919 these stalwart ladies were glad that the war was over and that they could return to their normal lives. Little could they suspect that in exactly 20 years time the job would have to be done all over again, and that the Women's Land Army would be called upon to make an even greater contribution.

Below: Now here's a little mystery. This is a photograph which we believe was taken at the 1935 Stafford Pageant. A group marching under the banner of the 'Masqueraders - Oldbury' are seen from the end of Glover Street, looking down Foregate Street. There's nothing unusual about a group of youngsters in fancy clothes taking part in a parade through the town, but who exactly were these 'Masqueraders'? We don't know; do you? Where were they from? There's an Oldbury in Shropshire, one in Warwickshire and yet a third near West Bromwich. In the exact middle of the 'hungry thirties' times may have been hard, but not so hard that people couldn't still find at least some time enjoying themselves. The girls taking part in this march past must be getting well on in age now, but perhaps a few of them are still around in the area and can tell us how where they were from and how they got on that day. A prize was awarded to the best-decorated entries. Along the route collections were made for Stafford General Infirmary; a valuable fund raising exercise in those days before the NHS came into being. The need for flag days and the like to support hospitals would come to a sudden end on 8th July 1948 when the NHS was inaugurated and new charities consequently became the focus of future fundraising. The annual procession through Stafford ended with a fair on the town common: we do hope the girls enjoyed themselves.

This photograph was taken on Corporation Street during the Stafford Pageant of 1930. As always the procession ended with a fair on the town common. A prize was awarded to the best-decorated entries. Quite what the slogan 'A Brighter Army' refers to is a puzzle. But perhaps it refers to the Salvation Army. Are the young folk with their decorated bicycles members of the 'Sally Army'? Since more than 70 years have elapsed since this picture was taken it's unlikely that many of those seen here are still around to tell us what was going on, though no doubt some of them are still in the area. But exactly who they are is in truth immaterial. Though the years may have rolled by the experience of childhood remains eternal: the two tots in the centre of this shot could have been filmed yesterday rather than in the years before the second world war. What happened to them in later life we wonder; did they grow up happily and continue to live their lives in Stafford? Did they eventually become mothers and fathers with children of their own; twenty years or more after they marched along Corporation Street did they proudly watch their own children take part in similar pageants in the 1950s and '60s? Are there grandparents, or even great grandparents, out there who, on seeing this picture, will recognise the scene and themselves, and happily recall the day when they were the centre of attention? We do hope so.

It may have been two years before the war, but the memory remains. Countless display cabinets still contain a reminder of what is going on in this photograph taken at St Michael's School. The year is 1937 and Stafford's Mayor Bagley, flanked on the right by the dark-suited figure of Councillor Goodhill, is handing out commemorative mugs to young pupils in celebration of the coronation of George VI. The crowning of a new sovereign was an exciting thought for young minds, though few of the youngsters in the schoolyard really understood the enormity of what had been happening in the run up to that unexpected event. For those who were aware of the abdication crisis the background was a simple love story, and one with a sad ending when the king was faced with a terrible dilemma: marrying the woman he loved or stepping down from the throne. Only in more mature years would the girls pictured here reflect more deeply on the extraordinary circumstances, and on the fundamentally flawed character of the man whose family knew him as 'David' and the world as the Duke of Windsor. Few children would worry about the troubled new king; a shy man with a speech impediment who found his unexpected role a heavy burden, but who nevertheless shouldered it unselfishly. Something these girls might have thought about however was the fact that the King had two young daughters just like themselves, the Princesses Elizabeth and Margaret Rose. Did they get mugs too?

Below: Pictured here in 1945, laying a wreath at the Borough War Memorial in Victoria Square, is Stafford's mayor, H Wallace-Copeland. The event had already been an annual one since the end of the first world war: the end of hostilities in 1918, an 'armistice', coming into force at the eleventh hour of the eleventh day of the eleventh month and being commemorated thereafter on Armistice Day, the 11th of November. The Borough War Memorial was unveiled in 1922 in memory of the Stafford men who had given their lives in the Great War. The statue of the soldier originally faced the railway station, the place from which many of the soldiers had departed. After the building of the new Crown Courts, the statue was turned to face St Mary's Church. Though happily the death toll of British servicemen and woman in the second world war was far less than in the mincing machine that the fields of Flanders became, this ceremony in 1945 was in some ways even more poignant than that which accompanied the war memorial's unveiling 23 years earlier. There was no delay to numb the sorrow of those who had lost loved ones. Since this photograph was taken Armistice Day has been replaced by Remembrance Sunday, honouring the dead of many wars and conflicts. But, no doubt as long as anyone then present remains, some will not forget this particular day in 1945 and the powerful emotions felt at the time: sorrow and triumph, bitterness and joy, sadness and pride.

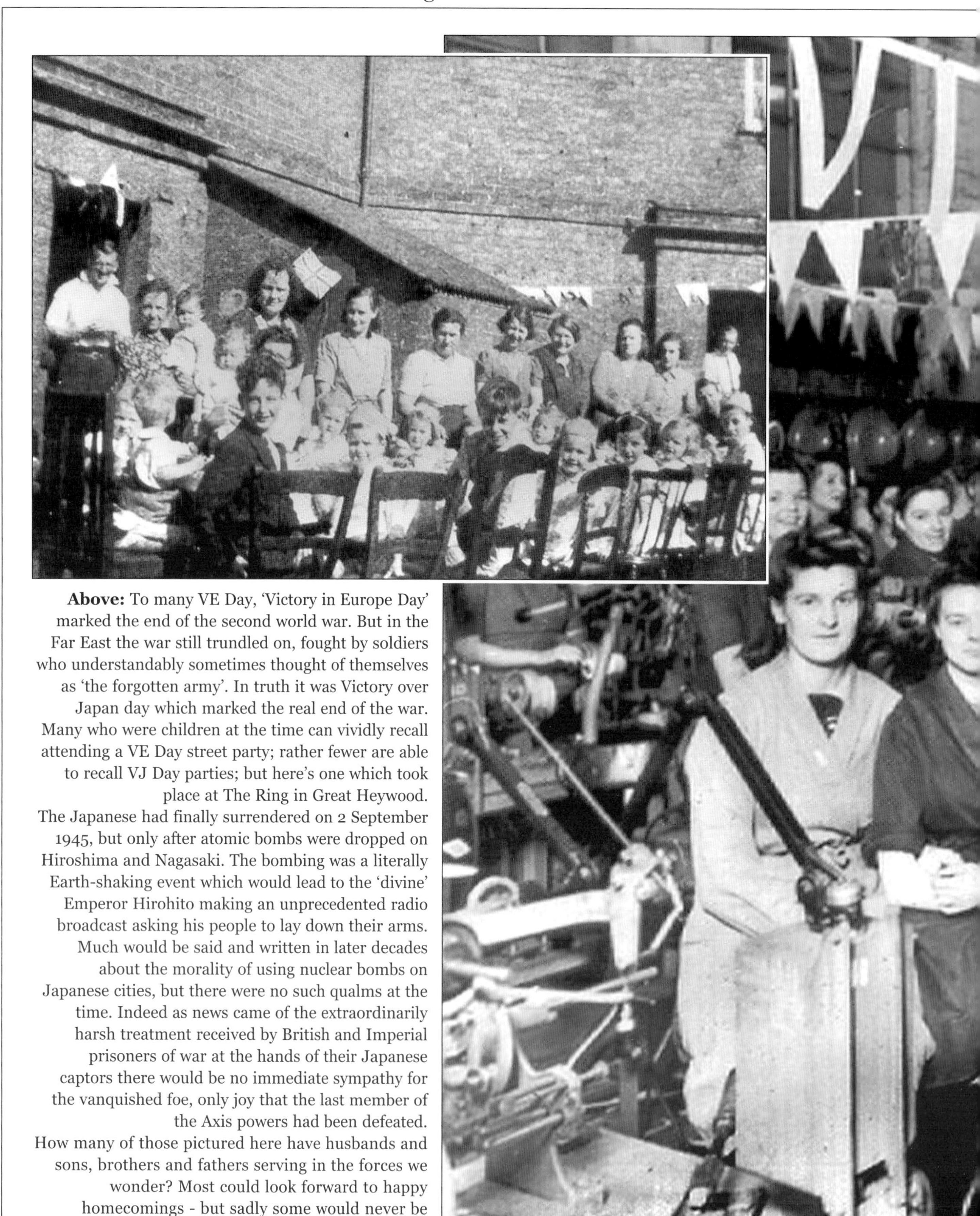

Above: To many VE Day, 'Victory in Europe Day' marked the end of the second world war. But in the Far East the war still trundled on, fought by soldiers who understandably sometimes thought of themselves as 'the forgotten army'. In truth it was Victory over Japan day which marked the real end of the war. Many who were children at the time can vividly recall attending a VE Day street party; rather fewer are able to recall VJ Day parties; but here's one which took place at The Ring in Great Heywood. The Japanese had finally surrendered on 2 September 1945, but only after atomic bombs were dropped on Hiroshima and Nagasaki. The bombing was a literally Earth-shaking event which would lead to the 'divine' Emperor Hirohito making an unprecedented radio broadcast asking his people to lay down their arms. Much would be said and written in later decades about the morality of using nuclear bombs on Japanese cities, but there were no such qualms at the time. Indeed as news came of the extraordinarily harsh treatment received by British and Imperial prisoners of war at the hands of their Japanese captors there would be no immediate sympathy for the vanquished foe, only joy that the last member of the Axis powers had been defeated. How many of those pictured here have husbands and sons, brothers and fathers serving in the forces we wonder? Most could look forward to happy homecomings - but sadly some would never be reunited with their loved ones.

'VICTORY' written large on the walls of the English Electric Company's Stafford factory says it all. The year is 1945 and here are several dozen female factory workers and a handful of men who are celebrating the long awaited arrival of peace at the end of World War Two.

On the outbreak of war in 1939 the company had switched to war work, exactly as it had done earlier in the century during the first world war. Formerly Siemens Bros., the company manufactured generators, electric motors and various other electrical appliances. During the war thousands upon thousands of women who, but for the war might have been content to be housewives, left their lives of domesticity to fight the war on the 'Home Front'. Millions of men had been called up to serve in the armed forces, but if they were to prevail the factories providing them with munitions and all the other material of war still had to be 'manned' by someone. Just as they had in the Great War women flocked to fill the workbenches. After both the first and second world wars the proof that women could do just as good a job as men served to hasten social change. Who could deny women equality? They had placed themselves in danger too: German bombers actively sought out factories contributing to the war effort and that very real danger is no better illustrated than by the sight of all those tin helmets hanging on hooks under the Victory sign.

Above: Though the Women's Auxiliary Air Force became the Women's Royal Air Force in 1948 it still didn't stop everyone continuing to refer to its members as WAAFs. And here we see a fine body of WAAFs marching along Stafford's Victoria Road in 1953 in a parade to mark Battle of Britain Week. Today, at least as far as civilians are concerned Battle of Britain Week seems to have gone the same way as many other important dates: whatever happened to Trafalgar Day or Oak Apple Day? Come to that what happened to Mafeking Day celebrating a long ago victory in the Boer War and once celebrated with such enthusiasm that the verb 'to Mafeking' became synonymous with partying? It seems sad to loose touch with our past when the events being marked are still well within living memory. The Battle of Britain took place between 10th June and 15th September 1940. German air attacks were successfully resisted by the young but incredible brave fighter pilots of the Royal Air Force, flying their famous

Top: Thirteen years after the event it is celebrating the RAF is marching along Victoria Road, Stafford during Battle of Britain Week. With its drummers to the fore the RAF is rightly proud to be feted by Stafford - and Stafford is rightly proud to fete them! The RAF had more than proved its worth every day during the six years of the second world war, but never more so than in the dark days of 1940 when only the miracle of Dunkirk had saved the British Army from annihilation and it seemed that only the young fighter pilots, scrambling into the air again and again in their Hurricanes and Spitfires stood between us and certain Nazi invasion. Of course being in the RAF was not just about war. And the word Royal in the name of the youngest of the armed services meant and still means being of direct service to Her Majesty.

The RAF had of course been prominent in the coronation of Queen Elizabeth II in Westminster Abbey on 2nd June, inevitably performing a spectacular fly past. The Queen's husband the Duke of Edinburgh had received his own wings as a pilot the previous month and his interest in flying may have contributed to the pair's decision to begin a six month tour of the Commonwealth, forsaking the Royal yacht and instead flying in the Stratocruiser Canopus. Not that Royal comings and goings held great interest for the small children watching the RAF march past; for many of them the key event of 1953 had been the ending of sweet rationing back in February.

Hurricanes and Spitfires and averting an invasion of Britain. Without the sacrifice made by those unforgettable young men Hitler's 'Operation Sea Lion', to transport a German Army across the English Channel would have become a reality. Fortunately the RAF prevailed, though not without many casualties. As Winston Churchill so aptly and accurately summed up the nation's gratitude at the time 'Never in the field of human conflict was so much owed by so many to so few'.

Gerald McCann

No prizes for guessing what's going on here. Yes it's prize-giving time at the Staffordshire County Show at Hopton. The year is 1960 and stepping up for a rosette and certificate is a fine looking dairy cow and her owner. For once the sun is shining brightly and the happy crowd is packed tightly into the stand behind the trophy table. But though the sun may be shining that hasn't encouraged the lady judge to discard her gloves - items of clothing still considered de rigueur for all respectable ladies.

Though the white coated dairyman and the two judges seem intent on discussing the excellent qualities which have led to the award of a prize we can't say that the cow seems to be taking to same interest. Perhaps she's spotted a prize-winning bull just out of shot and waiting for his award. If the poor cow has got her eye on a bull she's in for a disappointment. Artificial insemination had been 'invented' in 1785 by the Italian biologist Lazzaro Spallanzani: by the time this picture was taken such means of reproduction had become the norm and was leading to such phenomenal records as that of Bedalls Adema, a bull born in Dublin in 1964, and who, by his death 14 years later, had sired no fewer than 212,000 offspring. Whether the gentle looking bovine pictured here ever got anywhere near reaching the British milking record of over 25 tonnes of milk in a single year is, sadly, not recorded.

Below: 'Telephone Belles' was the float entered by the then GPO in the 1964 Stafford Pageant. It is seen here outside the Castlegate Telephone Exchange on Eastgate Street. The float was designed by Ian Tavernor.

For younger readers we'd best explain that GPO stood for General Post Office and that in those far off days before the great British Telecom privatisation the Post Office had the monopoly on running the telephone throughout Britain (well, except for Hull in what was then still the East Riding of Yorkshire, but that's another story). And perhaps again for the benefit of today's young people we ought to explain the witty choice of name for the float. Being a telephone operator, at least on the day shift, was in those days almost exclusively a female preserve. There was never going to be a GPO Beaux float.

Yes a belle is a beautiful young woman and of course young ladies from the GPO were going to ride on the float; but it's also a double pun. The telephone had been patented by the Scottish-American inventor Alexander Graham Bell in 1876 - but equally importantly telephones once had bells. Yes back in 1964 when a phone rang it did so quite literally. No doubt there are kids today with their mobiles and other electronic gizmos who find it hard to believe that once, not so long ago, you could not select any one of a hundred tinny electronic tones and jingles to announce an incoming call: the phone just rang.

At leisure

The three gables seen in the distance here belong to the Barley Mow public house where many a thirsty father has happily found temporary refuge, leaving his youngsters outside with straws stuck in bottles of lemonade and a packet of crisps to nibble. This photograph captures the Bank Holiday Fair on Milford Common in 1947. Milford was a very popular weekend destination for visitors in the late nineteenth and early twentieth centuries. Excursion trains ran between Stafford and Milford stations, later supplemented by fleets of private cars, charabancs and coaches. There doesn't seem to have been much order to the car parking arrangements; but then in 1947 there didn't need to be - there were few cars and lots of space. Road rage was still decades in the future. Here on Milford Common the closest anyone came to road rage was on the dodgems - always something of a misnomer since everyone tried to engineer the most spectacular crash possible. There had not been much in the way of candyfloss and ice cream for the generation brought up during the ten years which preceded this picture. But by 1947, though the government might have introduced a national austerity programme to help pay the debts accumulated during the war, people were fed up with being miserable and really wanted to enjoy themselves. True the fair rides may not have been quite as sophisticated as today, but what did that matter - those who had recently lived through the greatest war in history were savouring every moment.

Above: After the war many local companies encouraged their workers to participate in sports and social activities. In 1950 the English Electric Co. had a very strong sports and social club with a sports ground next to the works at The Hough, near Lichfield Road. And here's the English Electric Cricket team, and a few reserves. In fact there are 22 men here plus a couple of umpires in their white coats. Unlike later decades when full professional kit had become the norm for even the humblest of amateur sporting teams this photo emphasises the informality with which such teams played. Only one person in the frame is sporting a full kit of pads, a cricketing jumper and a bat; the remainder seem to have turned up in whatever they were wearing that day. But paucity in the clothing department was not reflected in the enthusiasm which they gave to the game. The dedication and enthusiasm of members and supporters of amateur sports clubs, in the days before television occupied so much of our leisure time, would put many of today's participants to shame, not least those who turned out for local cricket teams at a time when the sport was in its heyday. These really were golden years for English cricket. Just 12 years before this picture was taken hadn't we soundly beaten the Australians? In England's greatest ever victory Len Hutton hit 364 runs to help England beat Australia at the Oval by a staggering margin of 579 runs.

Above right: Do you recall happy afternoons spent paddling in Victoria Park? Or are your memories less happy after tripping up and falling in the water with all your clothes on? This photograph of the paddling pool was taken in the summer of 1950; how we enjoyed ourselves under the watchful eyes of our parents, and even more so when we thought they weren't watching and could kick the water to make the biggest splash we could. The large building on the left is Stafford Technical College. In the 19th century the land between Izaak Walton Walk and the railway station was marshy and liable to frequent flooding. In 1903 however the Stafford Corporation bought the land and raised its level by some three feet. Over the next five years the area was laid out as Victoria Park, which was officially opened on 15 June 1908. In 1911, to celebrate the coronation of George V, the park was extended across the River Sow towards Tenterbanks. A bowling green was added and the two parts of the park were linked by Coronation Bridge. The paddling pool, and a further extension, with tennis courts and a playground for children, were opened in 1930.
For children this may have been a carefree day, though for the adults sitting on the benches watching them it was a summer full of worries. North Korea had invaded the South and American and British soldiers had been sent in. A global conflict threatened, with China backing North Korea.

Right: This group photograph shows members of the Staffordshire British Friesian Breeders Club, outside their tent at the County Show at Hopton in 1959. For those who don't know it Frisia is an historic region of the Netherlands and Germany. Since the battle of Waterloo in 1815 it has been divided into Friesland, a province of the Netherlands, and the Ostfriesland and Nordfriesland regions of northwestern Germany. The Frisian language has gained ground in recent years and has been recognised as an official language of the Netherlands being taught in primary schools throughout Friesland. The Frisian people have become most famous for their cattle (records from as early as the 1st century BC suggest they already owned large herds of cattle); though they also

engage in other agriculture.
Improving the quality of British cattle has long occupied the minds of British farmers. The 20th century saw many systematic attempts to improve yields of milk as well as the quality of beef cattle. Friesian cattle were renowned on the continent and after the war large numbers were exported to Britain. Many impressive new herds were built up during the 1950s, not just of Friesians but also other breeds such as Jerseys.
As a result of such efforts numerous clubs were formed to share knowledge about new or unfamiliar breeds of cattle. Perhaps the most surprising thing about this photo however is, that despite farming being a traditional male preserve, eight out of ten of the club's members appear to be women.

Sparks of genius

Today it is hard to imagine a world without electricity. And the town of Stafford, through its long association with firms such as Siemens, English Electric, GEC and ALSTOM has probably done more than any other to turn the gas and candle-lit England of Queen Victoria into the neon-illuminated country it is in the 21st century.

The year 2003 marks one hundred years of electrical manufacturing at the Lichfield Road works in Stafford. It is an industry that has had a major effect on the fortunes of the town; indeed many houses were built by the early owners of the site. This story however begins even earlier than 1903.

It was in 1843 that the 19 year old Carl Wilhelm Siemens first came to England to sell his elder brother's invention for gold electroplating. Carl sold the invention to Elkingtons of Birmingham for £1,600, a considerable sum in those days. At that time there was no demand for electrical supplies and the brothers were mainly involved in the design and manufacture of telegraph equipment. In 1859 Carl established a factory in London's Millbank and in 1863 moved manufacture to Woolwich. The Siemens brothers came eventually to play a major part in both the manufacture and laying of transatlantic telegraph cable. Carl Siemens never returned to Germany and instead became a naturalised Englishman, changing his name to Charles William Siemens in the process: he was knighted in 1883 by Queen Victoria in recognition of his services to science but died the same year.

Despite the death of its founder the business continued to flourish. By the turn of the new century even the Woolwich site was becoming too small and a new site was being sought. Stafford was in the middle of the country and well served by roads. Furthermore the national railway had

***Right:** Siemens Dynamo Works, Lichfield Road, Stafford, viewed from Queensville Bridge c1903.*
***Below:** Siemens Stator Winding Gallery c1907.*

come to Stafford as early as 1837. The firm of Siemens Bros. bought 'The Hough', a 51 acre site, from Thomas Salt in 1901 and building work began. The 'Siemens Dynamo Works Limited', well served by extensive railway sidings and with rails actually leading into its buildings, opened in 1903. Some 800 workers were transferred there from Woolwich. The influx caused a local housing shortage and as a result the Salt Avenue 'colony' was quickly built (and extended again in 1924). Houses were also built in St George's Road in 1910 whilst in St Leonard's Avenue a new school was funded by the company.

As well as electrical machinery and switchgear some traction work was based in Stafford before it was transferred to Preston Works by English Electric in 1920. (Siemens Bros. had been connected with electric traction from its very early days, having equipped the Giants Causeway and Portrush Tramway in Ireland in 1883 - the first electric railway in the British Isles). Electric lamps were also made.

***Top:** Bagnalls Toolroom at the Castle Works c1925.*
***Above:** One of the first National Grid 132kV transformers c1926.*

Manufacture continued, although not very profitably, for some ten years before war with Germany threatened. At the beginning of the war in 1914, notwithstanding the founder's Anglicisation, the business was still owned by Germans; it was regarded as enemy property and seized by the government. Throughout the war years manufacture was directed to the war effort and armament manufacture; by 1916 around half of production was munitions.

The story leading to the 21st century is however not a straightforward one. The electrical industry in general has been remarkably incestuous. Additionally the industry's necessary rationalisation as competition has increased has encouraged the combination of many of the old companies. Much of the industry's early investment came from the USA, which wanted a foothold in Europe. British Westinghouse (Trafford Park, Manchester 1902, later to become Metropolitan-Vickers, always colloquially referred to as

Metro-Vick) and British Thompson Houston (Rugby 1902) were just two examples of this phenomenon; both would be amalgamated into Associated Electrical Industries (AEI) in 1928 and later absorbed into GEC as would be English Electric. (Thompson-Houston incidentally merged in 1892 with Edison General Electric to form General Electric of America, not to be confused with GEC).

The English Electric Company was formed from confiscated companies in 1918 and acquired the business of Dick Kerr & Co Ltd of Preston, Willans & Robinson Ltd of Rugby and Phoenix Dynamo Manufacturing Company Ltd of Bradford. In 1919 it bought the Siemens Bros. Dynamo Works Ltd at Stafford. Sadly the next ten years saw a general decline in both business and employment levels and by 1929 the company was in some difficulties. In the late 1920s, Westinghouse, having lost its links with Metro-Vick, was looking for new ways to maintain its interest in Europe and saw the ailing English Electric Company as its way forward. Westinghouse injected cash, something not in general knowledge at the time, and in 1930 appointed George Nelson as Managing Director of English Electric. George Nelson made Stafford the company HQ and years of prosperity now began.

In 1930, when George Nelson became Managing Director a trade agreement with Westinghouse was in place almost immediately. In 1933 as a direct result of that trade agreement English Electric began the production of domestic electricity meters to Westinghouse's design in the No. 28 shop in Stafford. That meter business, later moved to Stone, gave rise to instrument production in the period of the second world war, and after the war, in 1950 to relay production. Then known as the MRI Division (Meters, Relays and Instruments) of English Electric, it was spectacularly successful, and would eventually lead to the building of the St Leonard's works in 1960.

But that was still very far in the future when George Horatio Nelson was born in 1887. He was a brilliant student gaining a diploma at the London City & Guilds Technical College before his 18th birthday and winning a Brush Electrical Engineering Company studentship. Nelson became a premium apprentice at Brush's Loughborough works and was appointed Chief Outside Engineer when he was only 22 years old. In 1912 George Nelson had left Brush for British Westinghouse in Manchester. Eight years later the company, by now Metropolitan-Vickers, appointed him Works Manager over two factories in Sheffield recently acquired in its 1918 merger with Vickers. The new Managing Director of English Electric was a man

Top left *The Tank Shop, during World War II* ***Above:*** *Mk IX bombsight, made at the works during the second world war.* ***Right:*** *The visit of King George VI and Queen Elizabeth in 1942.*

of high principles, devoted to his country, the business and his workforce.

Within nine years of Nelson's appointment came the second war with Germany and its axis allies. And once again much of the company's production was directed to the war effort. As early as spring 1938 - quoting from 'The English Electric War Diary' - 'as a result partly of our personal observations on the Continent we felt that circumstances had arisen which made it the duty of this Company... to place its accumulated experience and engineering organisation at the disposal of the Government to help in this vital purpose of expediating the defence programme'. The first order for war material was placed on Stafford in March 1938: an order for overhead busbar equipment for a shadow aircraft factory. This would be the first of over 60 orders for similar equipment. An underground casualty clearing station was established in the works; it was equipped with air filtering equipment so as to be immune from gas attack and was capable of being used as an emergency operating theatre. Much emphasis was placed on staff welfare and this continued throughout the war years when there was a full time doctor, dentist and other medical staff on site.

There were discussions with the Air Ministry to ascertain what work could be done by the newly set up Meter Department and the following June this resulted in an order for Aircraft Engine Speed Indicator sets for Hampden bombers, which the company was building in Preston. These were to be the first instruments the company produced. Other precision instruments soon followed including the Mark IX course setting bombsights and repeater compasses. Buildings were extended by the government and the number of war effort products increased: these ranged from tanks of various kinds (over 1800 in all) to 2" mortar bomb tail fins and Mills bomb base plugs. In these years there were many visiting dignitaries to the site including HRH the Duke of Kent in 1940, General De Gaulle in 1941 and King George VI and Queen Elizabeth on 26th February 1942.

Above: *The National Grid's first 275kV Transformer installed at West Melton.* ***Below:*** *The same 275kV 120MVA 163 Ton Transformer emerging from Lichfield Road Works in 1953.*

Following the end of the war George Nelson, now Sir George, acquired the wartime building extensions from the government and continued to refine his research organisation. This was based in Stafford to serve the whole of the English Electric organisation and was known as the Nelson Research Laboratories (NRL). On their completion in 1946 the President of the Board of Trade, Harold Wilson, came to open the new laboratories. Further research facilities were set up at Blackheath to the east of Stafford, and in 1964 a new building, NRL Beacon Hill, was opened.

THE ENGLISH ELECTRIC COMPANY LIMITED
STAFFORD WORKS
Social and Athletic Association

President
J. Rogers
Vice-Presidents
H. M. Dyson M. Farrand
J. Jack E. Parkinson J. R. Sully
General Secretary
C. W. Whiteford

Programme of Events
for
Stafford Works
Sports Meeting
on
Stychfields Ground
Saturday, July 7th, 1951, commencing 2-15 p.m.

ADMISSION TO THE FIELD
On Payment at the Entrance Gates
ADULTS 6d. CHILDREN 3d.

Lists of Competitors will be available without charge at the Entrance Gates

J. & C. MORT, LTD., STAFFORD

Though the end of the war had meant the cancellation of aircraft orders Sir George decided to stay in the aircraft business and set his Preston design and development team to work on new projects. The long and expensive process paid off when on 13th May 1948 the first jet propelled bomber ever produced in Britain flew for the first time. The Canberra was the most advanced aircraft in the world, and the most successful British aircraft ever designed in peacetime. Before this English Electric had been almost entirely dependent on the market for heavy electrical goods, selling mainly to electricity authorities, railways and industrial companies. Now, to widen the company's horizons Nelson bought the Marconi company.

After the war there was a shortage of skilled labour. In order to address that shortfall the apprentice training scheme was stepped up. Soon there were as many as 1,100 apprentices in a workforce of 12,000. There was also a shortage of housing: George Nelson established the Kingsway Housing Association to address the problem. The English Electric Housing estate at Stafford's Burton Manor, built in the early 1950s, was one of its finest achievements and won awards for its design.

Meanwhile the MRI Division expanded and by 1955 was a separately accounted business. With George H Spratt as its manager expansion and profits increased so much that within five years a new £1,600,000 state of the art factory was being planned. The ultra-modern St Leonard's works, begun in 1960 was fully operational by 1962. The workforce in 1960 was over 800; that number would double in the five years which followed.

Top Left: *Measuring a Turbo Alternator Frame.* ***Top right:*** *Thorpe Hall, the Lady Nelson Convalescent Home.* ***Above right:*** *Machining a 60,000KW alternator rotor.* ***Above left:*** *English Electric's Sports Day programme from 1951.* ***Far left:*** *The Large Machines erection bay, Lichfield Road c1967.*

W.H. Dorman & Co, manufacturer of diesel engines in Tixall Road, acquired W G Bagnall's Steam Locomotive business at Castle Works in 1959, and was itself acquired by English Electric in 1961. When the diesel engine business was subsequently sold, Castle Works remained, but has now been sold.

George Nelson had been knighted in 1943; he became a baronet in 1955 and a baron in 1960 taking the title Lord Nelson of Stafford. Lord Nelson lived on site at 'The New Hough' for over 30 years until his sudden death in the corridor outside his office in 1962; he had regarded the workforce as his 'English Electric family' and paid great attention to its members' welfare and education. Lord Nelson's son, H George Nelson now inherited both his father's title and his company; he had been appointed Managing Director of Napier in 1942 when he was just 25 and in 1949 he had been made Deputy MD of English Electric. Five years after George Nelson's death AEI was taken over by GEC. In the following year H G Nelson was shaking the hand of Arnold Weinstock in agreement to a merger between English Electric and GEC.

Despite being the best run of the three main British electrical companies by the end of the 1950s English Electric was the one which had the most severe long-term problems. The cut-backs in defence spending by the government meant that English Electric's diversification into military aircraft was under pressure whilst the major proportion of its resources was still committed to heavy electrical products. The late Lord Nelson had attempted to move the company into lighter electrical engineering in 1960 by trying to arrange a merger with GEC but his overtures had been rejected at that time.

Arnold Weinstock had been appointed Managing Director of GEC in the same year as the old Lord Nelson's death. Following his discussions with the new Lord Nelson the government gave its approval on

Top right: *Lord (GH) Nelson, 1956.*
Above left: *Arnold Weinstock and Lord (HG) Nelson shaking hands over the merger of EEC and GEC in 1968.* ***Left:*** *Arthur Mowl and Clarry Benton working on a single disc polyphase meter, 1962.*
Below: *Pat Banks instrument scale marking, 1962.*

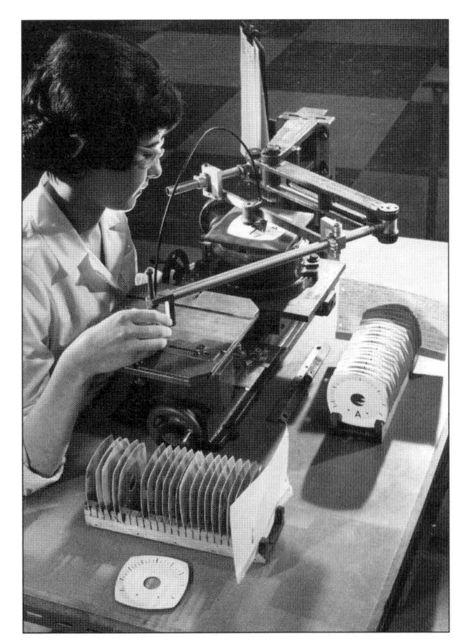

Friday 13th September 1968, for a merger between GEC and English Electric. The merged companies were at first known as The General Electric and English Electric Companies Ltd but some 12 months after the merger became simply GEC. In July 1969 the English Electric MRI Division became GEC Measurements.

These would prove to be difficult times. Following GEC's take-over of AEI in 1967 AEI's Woolwich telecommunications factory was closed down with the loss of more than 5,000 jobs. This had been the site, which Siemens had outgrown at the turn of the century and which had given rise to the creation of the Stafford Lichfield Road factory. There were further job losses within the AEI organisation. The announcement of the GEC/English Electric merger gave rise to a feeling of apprehension within the Stafford workforce.

St Leonard's works survived the merger relatively untouched by Weinstock's management style because it was a relatively young business in a new factory. Thanks to the foundations laid by its manager George Spratt, St Leonard's site had kept its finger on the business pulse and was able to readily adapt to Weinstock's efficiency measurement techniques.

Arnold Weinstock, who had been knighted in 1970, was made Lord Weinstock in 1980.

It was early in 1989 that Lord Weinstock set up a joint venture between GEC and a French company, Alsthom, to help GEC deal more easily with international markets. GEC Alsthom was formed as a jointly owned company with some 85,000 employees and a £4 billion turnover. As part of the new company GEC Measurements now became GEC Alsthom Measurements Ltd on 1st July 1989 and various organisational changes led to further modifications of its name: GEC Alsthom Protection & Control Ltd in 1991 and GEC Alsthom T&D Protection & Control Ltd in

Top left: *Stychfields Hall, 1967.* ***Top right:*** *Stonefield Meter Factory.* ***Above right:*** *The newly opened Nelson Research Laboratory, Beacon Hill, June 1965.*
Right: *Tap changer assembly at Castle Works, 1967.*
Below: *The new Transformer Works c1965.*

1993. GEC Meters, having moved to Stone in 1976 was not a part of the new company.

Lord Weinstock stepped aside from the company in 1996 becoming Chairman Emeritus when George Simpson was appointed Managing Director of GEC.

GEC Alsthom was floated on the stock exchange on 22nd June 1998 under the name ALSTOM. This would be a totally independent international company: the letter 'H' had been dropped following research amongst customers. St Leonard's works now housed ALSTOM T&D Protection & Control Ltd: turnover for the year would be £97.5 million.

Despite a century of extraordinary change one thing has remained constant: the company's ever increasing reliance on electricity and the equipment to generate, transmit, measure and control it. Electricity has been the major industry in the town of Stafford for a full century now and there can be no one locally whose life has not been touched by it. Today there are people in Stafford working the electrical industry at ALSTOM whose father's grandfathers and even great grandfathers worked successively for such great names as English Electric and GEC. But, in what has now been dubbed the 'Electronic Age', we should not forget those who have gone before us: not least that talented and entrepreneurial young German Carl Wilhelm Siemens who came to England and founded a company which would one day create employment for countless thousands of workers both in Stafford and all around the world.

ALSTOM today is a worldwide business with a turnover in excess of £14 billion and employing 112,000 employees in over 70 countries. £1.5 billion of this generated from 14,000 employees is in the UK with a substantial proportion of sales as exports.

Stafford's Lichfield road plant still makes power transformers and has recently built the four biggest transformers ever in Stafford. The 900MVA generator transformers were for a project in Malaysia. They weighed a massive 350 tonnes and were almost 12 metres long and over 5 metres tall. There is expertise in DC power links and ALSTOM is playing a leading role in building the national grid in India where regional AC systems need to be linked for power sharing. (There are technical difficulties in linking large AC power systems mostly due to synchronisation problems and DC links provide a solution.) ALSTOM supplied the largest (2,000MW) submarine high voltage DC power link in the world, the link between England and France. Only the rotors for generators are now manufactured.

St Leonard's Works continues to provide expertise in the application of its world-leading designs of protection and control relays for power generation, transmission and distribution plant.

Above left: *St Leonard's Works from the air c1977.*
Below: *Lichfield Road Works from the air, 1983.*

Wartime

Here we are in late 1940. Members of Stafford's Auxiliary Fire Brigade are being presented to the Duke of Kent in Market Square. Made up of volunteers the Auxiliary Fire Brigade's Green Goddess fire engines would still be a familiar, if rarely seen, part of the public services more than sixty years later.

Even without a caption it would be easy to deduce that this is a wartime scene, with a senior military officer on the left standing alongside civil defence volunteers wearing their steel helmets.

The men on parade, with their fire-axes on their belts, look proud to be receiving some Royal appreciation for doing their bit. And they certainly deserved some appreciation. This photograph was taken shortly after the men's return from Coventry where they had helped to fight the fires after the city was bombed in November 1940. Few who lived through that period will ever forget the event which gave the English language a new verb: 'to Coventrate'. Though that novel verb may not have survived as long as the German-derived word 'Blitz' the horrors of the fire storm which engulfed Coventry in just a few short hours would be etched in the memory of all who were witness to it: not least members of the fire services.

Indeed, for the fire services, Coventry was nightmare; one made far worse by the fact that German bombs had breached canal banks and at a stroke removed a major source of water for fighting the terrible conflagration.

Gerald McCann

Left: Back in 1941 a cameraman visiting Adbaston took a photo of this bonny pair. The young lady, pictured with her walking stick, Wellington boots and beret is a member of the Women's Land Army; the sharp-horned bovine she is standing next to is a hand-reared British Friesian heifer. The WLA had its origins during the First World War, called into being to help the nation deal with the inevitable food shortages that were the natural consequence of thousands upon thousands of male farm workers volunteering for Kitchener's Army in the sadly mistaken belief that they would all be home by Christmas. Someone had to fill the vacancies caused by the prolonged absence of all those men, and into that gap stepped the women of the WLA. The young women who enrolled had the choice of working in agriculture, timber cutting or foraging for animal feeds. The girls had to cope with exactly the same work which had been undertaken by men; who had worked in the farming industry: muck spreading, hoeing and harvesting, driving tractors and farm machinery. But in those far off days there were still as many if not more horses working on the land as tractors. Indeed even by the time the second world war came along in 1939 girls in the WLA were quite as likely to be dealing with horses as they were horsepower. In 1938, with war clouds looming over Europe, the Women's Land Army was reorganised; the organisation continued to exist until 1950.

Below: There was a time when IT stood for International Telegram. There was time when a man could send a post card from work to tell his wife that he would be late home because of unexpected over time. Once there was no need for first and second-class mail because all mail arrived within 24 hours of being posted.
But if even that was not fast enough you could always send a telegram. E-mail and faxes aren't really new; they are just the most recent manifestation of something which had already been around for exactly a century by the time this photograph was taken.
An American, Samuel Morse, had patented the electric telegraph in 1840 and the age of instantaneous electronic communication had been born.
Within a few decades the world was ringed by cables creating a Victorian Internet which connected Washington with London and Stafford with Shanghai. The dots and dashes of the Morse Code would arrive at local Post Offices and be transcribed into words before being despatched to their recipients, taken by bicycle and later by motorcycle; in wartime at least, being handed a telegram could strike terror into the recipients who hardly dared open the envelope lest the news be bad. The GPO, as the Post Office was then called, employed many young men, aspiring postmen, to run errands for it. Here captured on film for us in 1941 is local messenger boy, Clive Holt, aged just 14 and resplendent in his uniform complete with cycle clips.

Both pages: n 1939 Britain's Prime Minister Neville Chamberlain had made his announcement to the waiting people of Britain that '...this country is at war with Germany.' The country rolled up its sleeves and prepared for the inevitable. This war would be different from other wars. This time planes had the ability to fly further and carry a heavier load, and air raids were fully expected. Air raid shelters were obviously going to be needed, and shelters were built on open places across towns and cities.

By the time war was declared an army of volunteers of both sexes had already been recruited to form an Air Raid Protection service. At first ARP personnel were unpaid volunteers but when war broke out in September 1939 they became paid staff. It was their job to patrol specified areas, making sure that no chinks of light broke the blackout restrictions, checking the safety of local residents, being alert for gas attacks, air raids and unexploded bombs. The exceptional work done by Air Raid Wardens in dealing with incendiaries, giving first aid to the injured, helping to rescue victims from their bombed-out properties, clearing away rubble, and a thousand and one other tasks became legendary; during the second world war nearly as many private citizens were killed as troops - and many of them were the gallant ARP wardens.

At the beginning of the war Sir Anthony Eden, Secretary of State for War, appealed in a radio broadcast for men between 17 and 65 to make up a new force, the Local Defence Volunteers, to guard vulnerable points from possible Nazi attack. Within a very short time the first men were putting their names down. At first the new force had to improvise; there were no weapons to spare and men had to rely on sticks, shotguns handed in by local people, and on sheer determination . Weapons and uniforms did not become available for several months.

n July the Local Defence Volunteers was renamed the Home Guard, and by the following year were a force to be reckoned with. Television programmes such as 'Dad's Army' have unfortunately associated the Home Guard with comedy, but in fact they performed much important work. The Guard posted sentries to watch for possible aircraft or parachute landings at likely spots such as disused aerodromes, golf courses on the outskirts of towns, local parks and racecourses. They manned anti-aircraft rocket guns, liaised with other units and with regular troops, set up communications and organised balloon barrages.

Other preparations were hastily made. Place names and other identifying marks were obliterated to confuse the enemy about exactly where they were. Notices went up everywhere giving good advice to citizens on a number of issues. 'Keep Mum - she's not so dumb' warned people to take care what kind of information they passed on, as the person they were speaking to could be an enemy. Older readers will remember how difficult it was to find certain items in the shops during the war; combs, soap, cosmetics, hairgrips, elastic, buttons, zips - all were virtually impossible to buy as factories that once produced these items had been turned over to war work. Stockings were in short supply, and resourceful women resorted to colouring their legs with gravy browning or with a mixture of sand and water. Beetroot juice was found to be a good substitute for lipstick.

Clothes rationing was introduced in 1941, and everyone had 66 coupons per year. Eleven coupons would buy a dress, and sixteen were needed for a coat. The number of coupons was later reduced to 40 per person. People were required to save material where they could - ladies' hemlines went up considerably, and skirts were not allowed to have lots of pleats. Some found clever ways around the regulations by using materials that were not rationed. Blackout material could be embroidered and made into blouses or skirts, and dyed sugar sacks were turned into curtains.

TREBLE WEAR
SHOES
FOR BOYS AND GIRLS
25/11
29/11
36/9
BOWEN'S
FAMILY SHOES
M.A.R.S.U.
R.N.A.S. ABBOTSINCH
4208 RN

During the course of the second world war military transporters of all kinds were a familiar sight on Stafford's roads. Here, in a photograph taken in Foregate Street, and believed to have been taken in 1943, are low loader lorries transporting fighter aircraft fuselages.

In the midst of war such things had become sufficiently commonplace for pedestrians to hardly give these lorries and their loads a second glance.

After four years of conflict war planes, tanks, ships and munitions were pouring out of Britain's factories at an ever increasing rate as war production moved towards its zenith. Perhaps the lack of interest also reflects the fact that by now folk were far less worried about the eventual outcome of the war. After the early defeats and disasters we had been bolstered by Churchill's stirring words, and mightily relieved that thanks to the pilots who fought in the Battle of Britain we would not in fact have to literally 'fight them on the beaches' as most people had thought probable. By 1943 we were taking the battle to the enemy and Hitler's defeat was a certainty. The only real question was how long it would take us and our allies to do the job. The previous year the eighth army had defeated German and Italian armies in North Africa - a victory which marked the turning point of the whole war, though one which prompted Winston Churchill to later say of the over-jubilant General Montgomery 'in defeat, unbeatable; in victory, unbearable'!

It may have been raining heavily on the day this photograph was taken, but what a boon for the photographer who has managed to capture the reflection of the horses in the mirror-like surface of the road.

The three mounted policemen are leading a parade headed by the North Staffordshire Regiment.

The crowd in Market Square must run into thousands; not even the heavy rain has discouraged them. From the small number of umbrellas and the number of uncovered heads it is easy to deduce that on this day at least the weather forecast was badly wrong.

Quite what the occasion might be is something of a mystery. Archive records suggest that the scene was captured some time around 1940. There is certainly no doubting that this is a military parade, with troops marching past civic dignitaries and senior military officers who can be seen on the right of the picture. Quite possibly the photo commemorates the departure of members of the North Staffordshire Regiment for France early in 1940. War had been declared against Germany on 3rd September 1939 and British troops had begun arriving on the continent to support France by 11th September.

It would of course be too little too late. The German blitzkrieg or 'lightning war', spearheaded by panzer tank divisions, soon pushed all opposition out of the way. Only the remarkable evacuation of the British Army from the beaches of Dunkirk in June 1940 ensured that it survived to fight another day.

On the move

This lorry, loaded with pipes, isn't going anywhere for a while The accident in Foregate Street was captured by a cameraman in 1940. The mobile crane from the firm of Longton's looks positively primitive compared to the kind of equipment which would be used today; but for all its limitations the crane is getting on with lifting the lorry's load away from the building against which it is resting.

Lorry driving is still a difficult and dangerous job, but nothing like as hard work as it was back when this picture was taken. In the days before power steering and power assisted brakes lorry driving was a job that need strong arms to turn the massive steering wheels which were necessary to provide enough leverage to do the job. Dual-circuit pneumatic brakes and seat belts may have been improbable luxuries, and crashes common, but fortunately most were not fatal - lorries usually simply didn't travel fast enough. Only in the 1970s did newer, more powerful rigs enable fully laden lorries to thunder along at 70 miles per hour as a matter of course. Until then generations of motorists had become accustomed to crawling along behind lorries inching their way up hills whilst belching out clouds of diesel; they waited patiently until the kindly lorry driver stuck his arm out of the window and waved the grateful motorists past.

The building into which the lorry has crashed would incidentally, some eight years later, become the offices of the Stafford Hospital Management Committee.

Stafford's historic Market Square is pictured here in 1940. The square had been the site of a weekly market for centuries. In 1853 a covered market had been opened behind the new Guildhall; however, despite that state-of-the-art facility, some stalls still continued to trade from the Market Square. In 1927, in deference to the ever-growing number of motorists, the Borough Council removed the remaining stalls and turned the square into a car park. Even the Jubilee Fountain, which had graced the Square for many years, was removed in 1934 to provide extra space for cars. Indeed there were so many cars that special measures now needed to be taken to keep them all moving. On the left hand side of the frame can just be made out a traffic policeman with white arm bands directing traffic, a much valued task in those days before there were traffic lights on every corner. In its turn the car park would also eventually disappear, remaining only until 1953 when it was replaced by flowerbeds to celebrate Queen Elizabeth II's Coronation.

On the left is Mummery's jewellers shop, on the corner of Market Square and Gaolgate Street. The building was later demolished and replaced by a new building occupied by the Alliance and Leicester Building Society. In the centre, built in lighter stone, is the National Provincial Bank, which would subsequently become the premises of Pizza Express. On the right is Lloyd's Bank, occupying the former home of the Stafford Old Bank.

MIDLAND RED

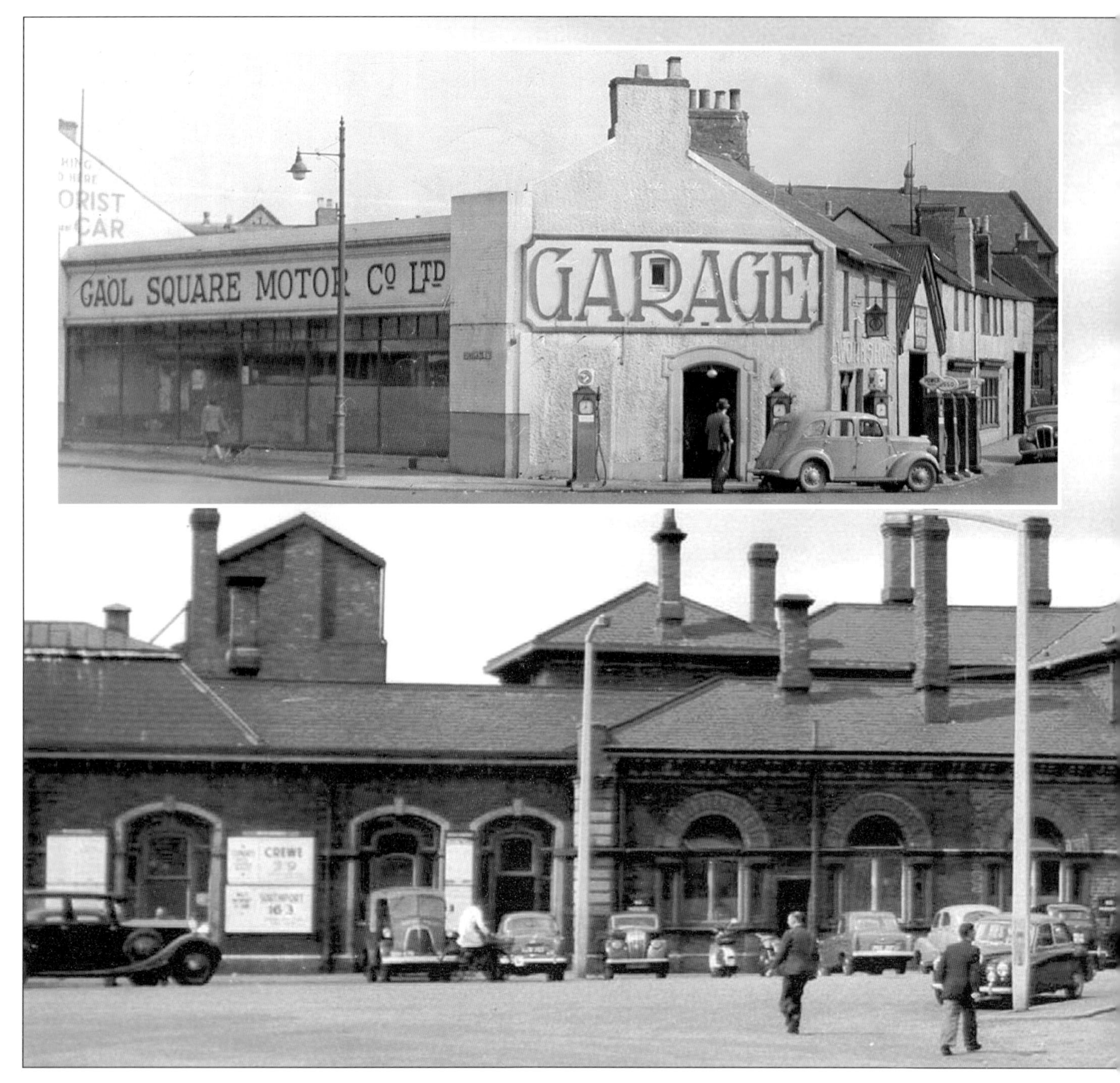

Above: Taken around 1950 this picture features the exterior of Stafford Railway Station on the left of the scene. On the right is the Station Hotel. The hotel on Victoria Road was originally called the North Western Hotel and was built in 1866, to provide accommodation for rail travellers. In its heyday the hotel provided all the latest facilities which included a coffee room reserved for ladies and a billiard room, whilst its kitchens were located on the second floor in order that its guests would not be troubled by cooking smells. A little over 20 years after this scene was captured the hotel was demolished. In place of the grand old hotel a motorcar salesroom would be built.
As for the station, that of course would long survive the hotel. The Grand Junction railway line had opened in July 1837. Within the next twelve years lines had opened from Stafford to Wellington and, via Lichfield to Rugby. The suburb of Castletown, en route to Doxey, were built to accommodate the railway workers. Stafford's original railway station was built in the early 1840s but was rebuilt in 1862. Back in 1950, when taking an aeroplane flight to our holiday destinations was the stuff of fantasy the recently nationalised railway was still the starting point for almost all long journeys. In those days, and for many years afterwards, it was still possible to have one's luggage collected by railway staff from home and to arrive at one's destination and find the suitcases already there.

Inset: Older readers will recall the garage of the Gaol Square Motor Company Ltd pictured here in 1949. What memories the scene invokes. No double yellow lines for a start, and no traffic wardens to enforce parking restrictions had they existed.
These were still the days when the motorist was treated like a king. All we had to do was pull up at the petrol pump and tell the attendant what we wanted and he would do the rest: we didn't even have to get out to pay. The downside in 1949 however was that petrol was still being rationed, an annoying fact of life and one which inevitably led to petty pilfering with many drivers waking up to discover that overnight their petrol tank had been siphoned empty. Theft was made all the easier by the fact that in those days no motor car manufacturer had thought to include a locking petrol cap as part of the standard specification.
In the half-century since this scene was captured on film motorcars have transformed our world; you'd have to get up very early on a Sunday morning to find a street in any town in Britain with so few vehicles in sight. At least we didn't take cars for granted back then: how exciting just to be given a ride in a car when so few people owned one. And how unpredictable when even before a journey of just a few miles it was wise to carefully check the water level in the radiator.

Here's Stafford Fire Station on Mill Bank pictured in 1950. Emerging from the fire station is a quite modern-looking fire appliance whilst a much older, open-topped fire-engine with its long ladders ending in huge wooden wheels, is seen on the left. In the distance a plume of smoke can be seen rising. We suspect that in 1950 the sight did not immediately give rise to frantic shouts of 'Help! Fire!' and that it is unlikely that these fire engines are about to race down the road with their bells urgently ringing. In those days before central heating and smokeless fuels the world was a far smokier place. Not only was virtually every household heated by coal but also most large buildings were heated by hot water from coal-fired boilers - and some factories still used steam engines to power their machinery. Chimneystack fires were a regular feature of a fireman's life in 1950. The chimneys of coal burning homes had to be swept regularly to reduce the build up of soot inside them. Those who saved money by neglecting that all-important bit of housekeeping could easily find that the soot would eventually ignite and make a 999 call necessary. Another frequent cause of fires was cigarettes, when far more people smoked than today. In the background can be seen a scaffolding tower from which the firemen have hung their hoses to dry. In earlier years the tower of the Brine Baths had been used for the same purpose.

Above: A fine group of firemen are seen here in 1970 standing outside the fire station buildings on Lammascote Road. And of course in those days we could still say firemen. After all, how could any reasonable person ever expect a woman to lift a 14 stone man over her shoulder and climb down a ladder? But times change: today's firemen and 'firewomen' are collectively known as fire-fighters. It's strange to think of all those 'esses' that seem to have all but disappeared from our language - whatever happened to actresses, authoresses and manageresses we wonder?

On this day, behind our all male cast, (at least one of whom is prominently displaying his traditional fireman's axe at his belt), are pictured two comparatively modern fire engines; and on the right, manned by two more firemen, is a much older model marked 'Ex Royal Aircraft Establishment'. The presence of a vintage engine suggests that this photo was taken at some kind of open day at the fire station.

The fire engine in the centre is, incidentally, clearly fitted with a bell not a siren. A bell had been the early warning system on police cars, fire engines and ambulances for many decades, at first rung by hand, and later powered by electricity. By the 1970s however the noise of traffic coupled with the very high speeds that emergency vehicles now travelled at made it essential for them to be equipped with high powered sirens to clear a path along our busy roads.

This view of Eastgate Street taken around 1970 is near the junction with Tipping Street. In the background can be seen the looming bulk of County Council Education Department building, a modern edifice built in the 1960s on what had earlier been the site of Diglake House. Over on the right is the entrance to Avarne Place. The double-decker bus heading towards the bus shelter at first looks not dissimilar to today's vehicles; it takes a second glance for us to be reminded how times have changed over the course of more than 30 years.

Just squint a little closer and you'll see that the bus driver is completely closed off from his (and it's a 99 per cent chance of it being his and not her) passengers. This was a transitional period in public transport. The now normal one-man (or person) operated bus was still a rare sight in 1970. In those bygone days the bus conductor was still familiar figure to all. 'Plenty of room on top' and 'Move on down please' were his chirpy calls, and he'd help harassed mums with arms full of shopping and toddlers to get a pushchair on and off the vehicle. And how many times did you apologetically say to the conductor 'Sorry I've nothing smaller' when proffering your bus fare, only to be met with a gleeful smile from the conductor and his cheerful response 'Sorry I've nothing larger' as he gave you your change in what seemed like your own weight in copper coins?

Coca-Cola
FISH & CHIPS

Shopping spree

Gaol Square has undergone many changes down the years. This is a view looking down Gaolgate Street towards Market Square and was captured by the camera in 1950. On the right, behind the clock, is Sidney House, once occupied by Radio Rentals and the birthplace of Thomas Sidney once Lord Mayor of London. Though above shop window level many of the buildings would remain unchanged, in the ensuing decades almost all would have their shop fronts altered, many more than once. The group of shops on the right however have today disappeared completely, demolished in the name of progress to improve the roads.
Not that anyone in Gaol Square in 1950 would have anticipated the need for bigger, better roads. Life in the years immediately following the second world war was decidedly more leisurely than it would become even five years later. With more pedestrians and cyclists using the road than cars this tranquil picture suggests that Stafford was a very sleepy town indeed, something which was not quite as true as it appears.
If the clock is correct this ought to be the start of Stafford's 'rush hour' but the scene we see doesn't seem to match our present day experience of that term. A casual observer might assume that this the picture was taken on a Sunday, but the blinds out on the shops makes it clear that this is without question a weekday.
Sadly petrol rationing came to an end in 1950 - and with it went such tranquil scenes.

J E C Peters

Above: A different view of Gaolgate opposite its junction with Salter Street is one offered by this photograph taken in 1961. The ornate facade of the former Empire Hotel can be seen on the far right. From the comparatively quiet years of the 1950s, and with the national economy now booming, the volume of motor traffic has mushroomed as evidenced by this nose to tail traffic jam. There were already plans for some kind of ring road to be built around the town centre to alleviate the strain, and some hope that a new fangled motorway would take some of the traffic away from Stafford. The nearby stretch of the M6 would in fact be opened in the following year by the Minister of Transport, Ernest Marples and bring some temporary relief to Stafford's main streets. But back then not even the most pessimistic of prognosticators could have placed a bet on just how temporary that relief would be, and just how jam-packed even that new super highway would eventually become. Had such doom mongers wanted to place a bet however they would at least now have been able to do so. Until 1961 off-course betting had been illegal - though that had not prevented it happening, with many punters placing bets on races using illegal bookies' runners. In May 1961 however, under the provisions of the Betting and Gaming Act, bookmakers could set up shops anywhere. As a result betting shops quickly became a familiar feature of Stafford Streets.

It's Christmas in 1960. This photograph records one of the first years in which Stafford's town centre was decorated with festive lights for the holiday season. The view is of Bridge Street, looking towards the Market Square; on the right is the tower of the Royal Brine Baths.

Depending on your point of view this was either one of the last Christmases 'like they used to be', or one of the first of what they have since become.

The year 1960 marked a turning point in history. In the 1950s youngsters were largely content with gifts such as the latest Enid Blyton book or a Meccano set. A five-shilling Postal Order from a maiden Aunt and a Beano Annual were the kind of present that anyone would be happy with. But with increasing affluence and the insidious effect of television advertising the demands on parents' wallets were suddenly far more shrill than they had been before. But let's forget the 'need' for the latest computer games and mountain bikes and look back to that gentler era. Let's think back to long ago Christmas Eves when we tried to stay awake to see Father Christmas arrive, and always failed. Let's recall the Christmases when boys who received a torch for a present would use it to hide under the blankets and secretly read about Biggles or Billy Bunter before falling asleep dreaming of what life would be like when they grew up to be 'Pilots of the Future' like Dan Dare.

Above: This 1964 picture is taken from inside the 'new' Woolworth's shop on Gaolgate Street: John Collier's draper's shop window can be seen opposite through the glass doors. The "Pick 'n' Mix" counter at Woolworth's at 9d a quarter was proving highly popular. Don't ask us to tell you how many grammes there are in 4 ounces - a quarter of a pound - but, for the post-decimal generation, 9d is a little under four pence in today's money. Woolworth's was one of Stafford's few large stores. It and Marks and Spencer's were still one of the few chains, which could be found in the high street of almost every town in England. With its bright lights and open displays Woolworth's was a magnet for shoppers and petty pilferers alike. How many criminal careers began by surreptitiously filching a toffee from the pic 'n' mix counter we wonder. Fortunately the vast majority of the thousands of tiny terrors who succumbed to temptation later felt sufficient shame to forsake the possibility of more dramatic crime. Perhaps too the thought that crime doesn't pay would have been heightened by the knowledge that, like the Canadian Mountie, the British Bobby too generally got his man. The previous year a gang of audacious thieves had succeeded in halting the Glasgow to London mail train and got away with £2.5 million. The subsequent hunt for, arrest and trials of the perpetrators, not least the renowned Ronnie Biggs, would make newspaper headlines for years.

Right: This fine block of shops in Gaolgate is pictured here in 1962. Evidence of the town's ongoing development is clear on the gable end of the building where the 'ghost' of another structure can clearly be seen. The single car in view belies the fact that by now Gaolgate had become a very busy thoroughfare. Maybe on this day all the car drivers had gone for a spin on the newly opened M6. With few large stores, Stafford's shopping centre was still dominated not by national names but local ones
What would those people walking along the pavement have replied if they had been told that one day shopping malls and out of town superstores, accessible only by car, would be the order of the day? 'Not in my lifetime they won't' would probably have been the reply - but how wrong they would be. At least by now shoppers did have money in their pockets and things in the shops to spend it on. Three years earlier Prime Minister Harold Macmillan had told us that we'd never had it so good. And for once a politician was telling the truth. Real income had crept up during the 1950s and by 1962 Britain was riding a wave of unprecedented economic growth. The age of consumerism had been kicked off with the advent of ITV and the novelty of advertising on the airwaves. There was a distinct smell of optimism about, and with the Americans having recently put a man into space anything seemed possible.

J E C Peters

Above: No these aren't giant cotton reels but drums of electrical cable ready to be laid in Market Square just a few years before the first world war. Roadworks are nothing new it seems, though with far fewer cars about, and a much slower pace of life, digging a few trenches probably caused a lot less of a nuisance than it does today. Though this photo was taken around 1910 an electric works had opened on Bull Hill in 1895, from where just 36 shops and houses were supplied. Digging the roads up was not new even then: gas, water and sewers had already been hidden under the road surface. Indeed the existence of a perfectly good gas supply prompted many to ask what was the point of creating more disruption for something that had very little use.

In 1910 such doubters had a valid point. What could you use electricity for? There were no televisions or video recorders, power tools or dishwashers. The answer to that question was that domestic electricity supplies were mainly used for lighting. Some however said that the harsh light from electric bulbs was bad for the eyesight in comparison to the weaker, but mellower, light from gas mantles or even candles. Others worried that electricity was dangerous - unlike gas you couldn't smell it when it was leaking. Demand however continued to rise, and with it the range of domestic appliances, devices such as the electric iron, perfectly designed to plug easily into a light socket.

Making a living

All change. The year is 1934 and construction workers have moved into Market Square to make some serious alterations to Stafford's civic scenery.

The object of the workmen's attentions is Stafford's old Guildhall which is in the process of being demolished. The improvement, or desecration, depending on your point of view, was part of the Borough Council's plans to develop Market Square. A new Guildhall would be rebuilt further back from the square, and the market replaced by a shopping arcade. Though it might be assumed that the older Guildhall was centuries old, it had in fact only been erected in 1853, just 81 years earlier, an event then still perhaps within the living memory of the town's very oldest inhabitants. The building had housed the Borough Council and the courts, whilst on the ground floor was a police station. By the 1930s a new police station was needed and one was built on the corner of Bath Street and Albion Place. This photograph also neatly illustrates an important part of the history of the first half of the twentieth century: namely that the introduction of the internal combustion engine in the 1890s did not sound the immediate death knell of horse drawn transport. This scene, mixing lorries, cars pedestrians and a horse and cart, is a fairly typical example of what could be seen anywhere in Britain at the time. In fact it would take until the early 1960s before horses would have entirely disappeared from our streets.

J E C Peters

Above: Even for 1935 when this photograph was taken £10 for a cruise seems cheap. Perhaps the P&O shipping line was cutting its prices in order to attract custom at the height of the great economic depression which saw millions thrown on the dole. But if millions were trying to scratch a living below the poverty line at least this pair of young men seem to have found something to smile about. It's an ill wind that blows no good, and perhaps business was booming in view of the large number of bankruptcies. The shop in Salter Street belongs to the firm of George Horne & Son Auctioneers and Valuers. Anyone wanting to pop in for a chat about selling a house could do so with complete privacy thanks to the net curtains spread inside the window. For those who had money to spend, buying property then would never be so cheap. The idea that an ordinary house might one day fetch more than a hundred thousand pounds was inconceivable in a world in which a decent home could be bought for just a few hundred pounds and a run down cottage for far less. Meanwhile holiday cruises would remain nothing but a fantasy for the vast majority - though all too soon many young men would unexpectedly find themselves in far flung parts of the world. In the previous year the German President Hindenberg had died enabling Chancellor Adolph Hitler to successfully combine both positions to make himself an undisputed dictator.

Right: Lotus had previously been Edwin Bostock's shoe factory; earlier it had been located on Foregate Street, Stafford. That factory was destroyed by a disastrous fire in 1901 but had been rebuilt on Sandon Road in 1903. The Bostock Company had become Lotus Ltd in 1919. Here we are in the 'closing' department at Lotus, room where various leather shapes were stuck together to form shoe uppers. It's 1937 and the department is decorated for the Coronation of George VI: all the flags and banners were made by the factory girls themselves. It had not been a happy period for the Royal family. The previous year had seen three monarchs on the throne of Britain. George V had died at the beginning of the year and was succeeded by his eldest son King Edward VIII. To the astonishment of much of the British public Edward had abdicated after a mere 325 days. He had 'handed in his notice' because as King, and therefore head of the Church of England, he could not marry the women he loved - Wallace Simpson an American divorcee. The consequence of that abdication would be the succession to the Crown of Edward's younger brother as George VI, whose coronation is being celebrated here. Though many felt sympathy for Edward, now Duke of Windsor subsequent history, not least the eventually crowning of George's daughter, the much-loved Queen Elizabeth II, would make most folk conclude the right choice was made. The Lotus factory in Sandon Road was demolished in 1997.

1937

This photograph looks as if it was taken in Brook Hall, the Lotus factory canteen. It records the firm's 1965 Annual Conference dinner. It's strange how men's formal dinner attire has hardly changed in the four decades since this picture was taken. Indeed, despite the vagaries of fashion, the same formal clothing had been current for the previous six decades: the Tuxedo taking its name from the Tuxedo Park country club in New York where the jacket was first worn in the late 19th century. Nor, despite our recollection of short back and sides being popular in this period, at least amongst those no longer in their teens, do the men's hairstyles seem particularly dated.

By contrast women's fashions, both in clothes and hair, have undergone many changes since the evening that these dinner guest were caught on film. Gone are the tight perms and flyaway glasses, a style still favoured in the 21st century only by Dame Edna Everage. And gone too are the full and flowery dresses, then popular with the ladies, in favour of today's svelte and sophisticated styles. But what's on the menu for this grand occasion? In 1965 it's not likely to be fancy foreign stuff or vegetarian that's for sure. Few if any concessions were then made to 'eccentrics' be they vegetarians or religious or ethnic minorities who might have different dietary requirements to the majority. The choice was most likely roast beef, roast pork or roast chicken - and if that didn't suit then tough!

Gerald McCann

Above: The British Reinforced Concrete Engineering Company had moved from Manchester to Stafford in 1926, building a new factory in Queensville where it manufactured reinforced concrete structures as well as steel mesh for reinforcing concrete. There's not much concrete in sight here at the works canteen however. The two cooks working at the stove have their work cut out to feed a workforce, which in 1943 when this picture was taken, was working in an industry whose products were in great demand. From one end of the country to the other reinforced concrete shelters and pill boxes had sprung up like mushrooms as part of the effort to both protect civilians from German bombing as well as to provide strong points in the event of Nazi invasion. Fortunately by the time this scene was captured the threat of German invasion had receded as Hitler's ambitions had already switched from the English Channel and his ill-fated 'Operation Sea Lion' to the even more ill-fated 'Operation Barbarossa' - the invasion of Russia. Meanwhile back in Stafford it was business as usual in the works canteen. Though in many respects life as a cook has hardly changed there are at least a couple of features here that have disappeared from our lives: wooden tables have been replaced by more hygienic laminate and stainless steel work surfaces, whilst the milk churns are something that you now need to be middle aged to recall. During the 1980s concrete business declined and the factory closed in 1990.

In the carefree and sometimes careless days before the Health and Safety at Work Act came into force there were many more works initiation ceremonies than there are today. This particular ceremony, captured for posterity in 1953, was known as 'trussing the cooper'. It wasn't quite so strange as it sounds, nor quite so dangerous; but it certainly was messy. The scene is Joule's Brewery in Stone and records the 'passing out parade' for a former apprentice who has just finished doing his time. The newly qualified cooper was placed in a wooden barrel, which he had made himself. The barrel was then filled with a mixture of soot, feathers, shavings, beer and treacle. The barrel was rolled around the workshop by older colleagues, following which the new cooper was taken out and tossed in the air three times before being formally presented with his indentures. All the men standing around seem pretty pleased, but we bet the apprentice's poor mother wasn't smiling come washday! But this is one scene that is unlikely ever to be repeated. Not only has safety legislation put a damper on such ceremonies but apprenticeships themselves have virtually become a piece of history. Those that do exist certainly no longer involve signing impressive documents like indentures. And as for wooden barrels, yes they are still made, but hardly in the kind of numbers which were used in 1953: since this photograph was taken the aluminium cask has all but displaced the traditional wooden cask.

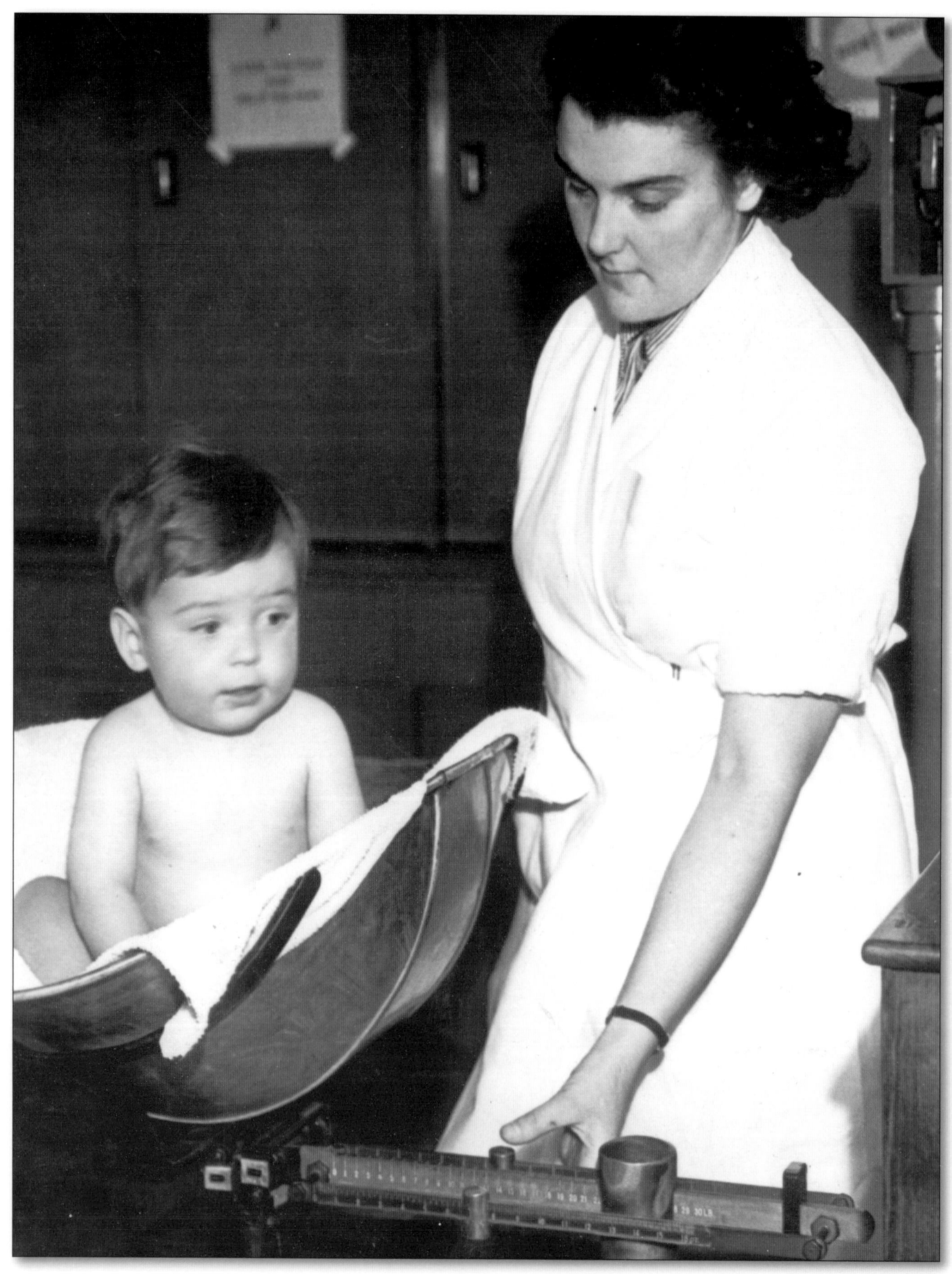

Both pages: It was possibly the acute wartime shortages of food and supplies which made doctors, health workers and mothers alike very aware of the health of the new generation, and children were carefully weighed, measured and immunised against the illnesses that had at one time meant disfigurement or even death (facing page). A vaccine for polio, the scourge of former years which left behind its terrible mark of wasted and useless limbs, only came later, however. American scientist Jonas Edward Salk developed a vaccine in 1955, and an oral vaccine was produced in 1960. The vaccines brought the dreaded disease under control and today polio is rarely seen. On a day to day basis, vitamins were vital to the health of children, and long before the advent of the cod liver oil capsule, the recommended spoonful of cod liver oil was administered to the youngest children every day in schools and nurseries around the country during the 1940s. Children might have screwed up their noses at the fishy taste, but the nourishing cod liver oil went a long way towards keeping them healthy. The vitamin-packed orange juice was far more palatable, and artful mothers would often use the orange juice as a bribe: no cod liver oil, no orange juice. Following hard on the heels of the oil, the juice took away the distinctive taste that was disliked by so many children. Ante-natal clinics did all they could to check on the diet, blood pressure and vitamin intake of mothers to be; our carefully posed photograph, taken in an ante-natal clinic in the 1930s, records at least the cleanliness and tidiness that was to their great credit (bottom). And when the tiny new citizen finally arrived, there were health visitors to pay friendly calls on families in their homes to check on the health and happiness of mothers and babies (left). National Dried Milk for babies was also made available to mothers, and before today's push towards natural feeding NDM was for decades very much in vogue. We need to remember that at the time of these photographs the National Health service did not exist, and in fact the NHS only came into operation after World War II in July 1948.

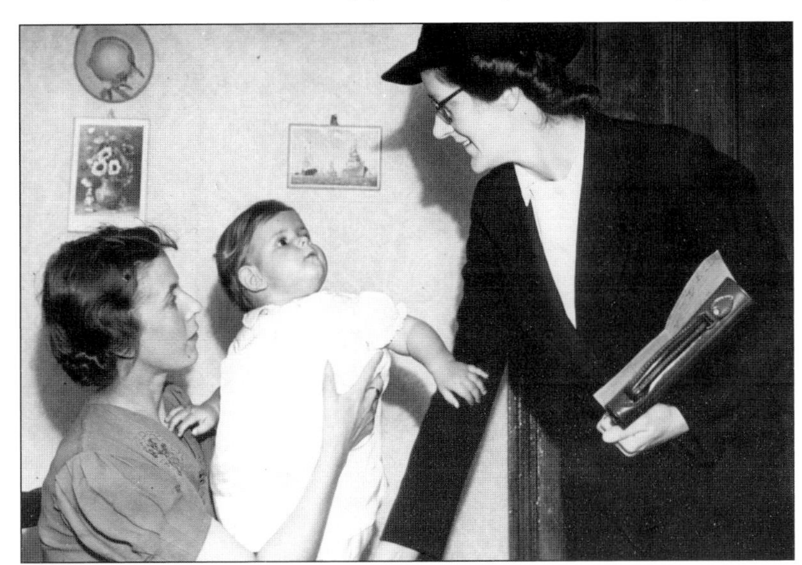

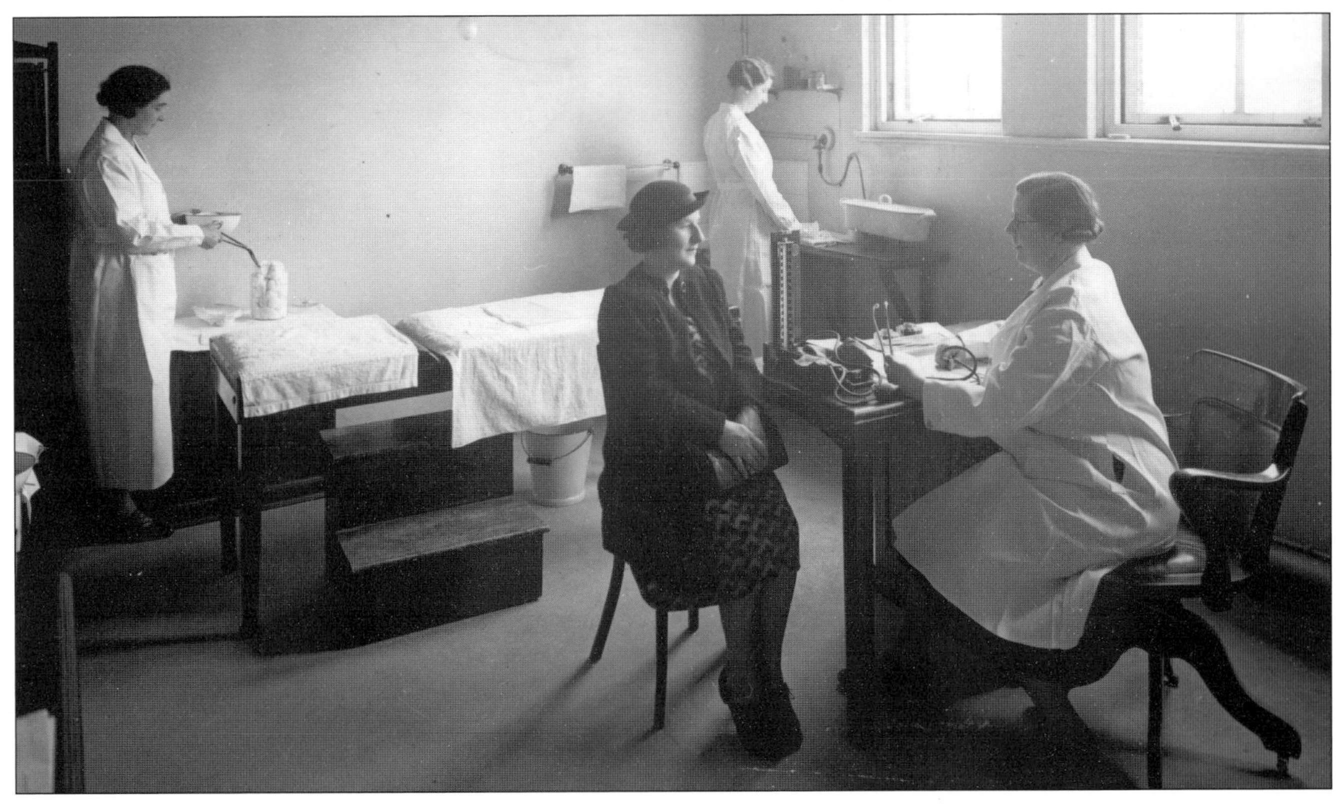

Below: Henry Mercer's saddler's shop once stood at the junction of Greengate Street and Mill Bank. In this scene snapped in 1962 The Baths Hotel can be seen on the left: to the right, on Mill Bank, is the Telephone Exchange.
The council had purchased Mercer's shop in the 1920s, along with various other buildings between the shop and the Coach and Horses public house. The reason for the compulsory acquisition had been the intention to widen Mill Bank - though what with council spending cuts, war and national reconstruction intervening it would take many years for the project to finally come to fruition. Certainly nothing in this photograph gives a hint that road widening was an urgent necessity.
Given that so many changes have taken place in Stafford in the post-war years it is remarkable that so much has managed to survive when planning blight in the 1960s managed to do more damage to Britain's architectural heritage than the Luftwaffe. Few towns would be as fortunate as Stafford which, in spite of a great deal of redevelopment, road building and demolition, happily still managed to retain enough of its older buildings to preserve its unique character. During the eventual demolition of Mercer's the lower courses of Stafford's old town walls would be revealed; today what's left of those ancient walls is now under the road surface of the present Mill Bank - but, needless to say, there is nothing left of Mercer's Saddlers Shop for future generations of archaeologists to excavate.

Bottom right: Who wouldn't immediately be tempted to go and buy some two-wheeled transport on seeing these four Motorcycle Mecca's shop assistants sat on their scooters?
The premises housing Motorcycle Mecca, on Market Street, were formerly a tea merchants and Oriental plaster figures still decorated its roof. This photograph was taken in 1960 when scooters, imported from Italy, were beginning to become a fashion statement as well as a cheap and practical form of transport for those who could not afford a car. One of the most popular and well remembered names would be Vespa - a marque which took its name from the Italian word for wasp; the name referred to the sound they made - a fact much seized upon by those who wished to denigrate this new form of transport in contrast to the deep manly roar of British motor bikes such as BSA and Triumph. But, manly or not, this form of transport was to sell by the million. Over the next few years scooters would be adopted as a symbol of the young 'Mods', as opposed to the 'Rockers' who retained an affection for black leather and motorcycles. The mods embraced the new: scooters were symbolic of novelty and would soon become an enduring image of the 'swinging sixties'. Scooter riding mods wearing their regulation fur-trimmed, hooded parka jackets, and still legally unencumbered by the need to wear crash helmets, would become a commonplace sight on Stafford's streets, and in every other town and city in Britain too.

Top right: In Stafford's Market Street and outside the premises of Motor Cycle Mecca, it is the summer of 1940. It's not motorcycles that are the focus of the photographer's attention but the roof-line above.
The oriental figures, looking down on passers by, date from the eighteenth century. The unusual

statues had been staring out over Stafford for many a long year, indeed from a time well before the internal combustion engine and pneumatic tyres had been thought of. In a much earlier incarnation the building had been a tea warehouse and the statues advertised that product. In two centuries of perching on the rooftop the long-lived figures had seen untold number of Stafford folk pass by in the street below them; they had watched red coated soldiers march off to fight Napoleon in the early 19th century, and seen the same red coats on their way to the Crimea in the middle of the century. In 1940 the red had been replaced by khaki and soldiers who were walking below had recently been evacuated for Dunkirk. How many of them we wonder looked above them and paused to consider that a lot more trouble would be coming their way from the Orient? Made from a hard plaster known as 'Roman Cement', the figures were a form of advertisement at a time when tea was an extremely expensive commodity.
When the premises were demolished in 1963 the famous figures were carefully removed and found their way to the County Museum collection at Shugborough.

On track for mortgages

A lady once deposited £500 with the Stafford Railway Building Society. Some months later she returned and withdrew £200. On carefully examining the notes however she complained that they were not the same bank notes she had deposited with the Society when she had opened her account! That was certainly one person whose concept of a risk free investment was as literal as it is possible to be. But the expression 'safe as houses' has not become proverbial without a reason. In the long term nothing has been such a good investment for ordinary people as buying their own home: something which folk in Stafford have been doing for a very long time indeed.

The Stafford Railway Building Society was founded and incorporated in 1877 by local townspeople and the Directors of the London & North Western Railway Company, whose main office was then in Stafford. Most notable amongst the 'locals' were Henry Venables and Frederick Espley, whilst the Mayor of Stafford was one of the first Trustees as well as being appointed as the 'Members' Auditor'.

From the outset the new organisation was a 'mutual' building society, that is to say one run by and for its members rather than shareholders. At that time however profits were specifically distributed to subscribing members who had to pay a membership fee. The new building society enabled the ordinary people of Stafford to buy their own homes by offering a low mortgage rate for borrowers and a fair and good interest rate for savers. But it was not just Stafford people who benefited: mortgages were made available to people all over the country, especially to employees of the railway, whilst the very first mortgage in fact went to help the Stafford Mechanics Institute (later Stafford College) buy premises.

Initially the Secretary's Office was based at the railway station but subscriptions were received at St Thomas' Schools in Derby Street each month, with two Directors present. The Secretary's Office moved to St Mary's Grove in 1890 whilst the Society still continued to receive subscriptions in Derby Street until 1927. The

Above: *George Dean, Secretary 1892.*
Below: *First Office, Stafford Station.*

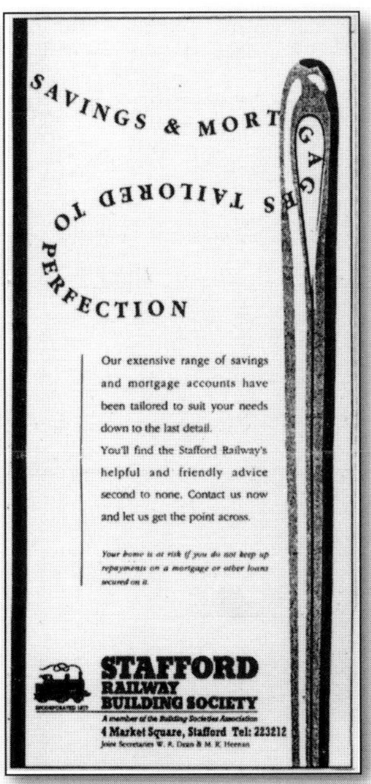

Society moved into its present offices at 4 Market Square when the William Salt Library moved out.

During the second world war there was serious disruption to housing activity and little new business was transacted during those years. The housing boom which followed World War II however helped all building societies to grow and the Stafford Railway Building Society, to the satisfaction of both its members and Directors, was no exception.

The Board of Directors has met monthly throughout the existence of the Society to supervise its affairs. Many distinguished local professional and business people have been directors of the Society over the decades with its Chief Executive at the start of the new millennium, Michael Heenan, having previously been Mayor of Stafford and Leader of the Council.

Since incorporation back in 1877 the Society has been managed on a day to day basis by accountants, initially from the London & North Western Railway (Messrs Illife & Fairhead) and then from 1892 by George Dean who had originally been an employee of the Railway Company and a Director of the Society, but by then left to set up his own accountancy practice. There then followed the long connection with the Dean family and the partners of the accountancy firm Dean Statham (formerly Dean & Son), a connection which continues to this day.

As we all know 'small is beautiful', though the Stafford Railway Building Society may be beautiful these days its smallness is only relative. From modest beginnings in the reign of Queen Victoria the assets of the Society would grow throughout the course of the 20th century - from £77,000 in 1927 to £9 million by 1977 - and in the opening years of the 21st century exceeding £90 million, whilst reserves which were a mere £2,000 in 1927 had grown to £750,000 by 1977 and swollen to a massive £6 million by the Society's 125th anniversary in 2002. Though much of that growth would be a reflection of the increasing prosperity in Stafford it would also reflect the attractiveness of the Society to investors and borrowers further afield: today some 40 per cent of lending is outside Staffordshire.

Meanwhile, though well known in Stafford, the only drawback to the historic name is that confused foreign visitors still come into the Society's offices to ask when the next train is leaving for London.

Top: *The Society's Office since 1927.*
Above left: *Advert for mortgages, 1933.*

In fact, although the Society is still referred to by many locals as 'The Railway', it no longer has any connection with the rail transport industry - apart that is from the image of the steam locomotive which serves as the Society's logo.

But though some things may have changed with the passing years, others have not. The Society remains as strongly committed to mutuality as ever. It is still run for the benefit of its members rather than any shareholders. That commitment is demonstrated by treating all its members alike and offering all its services to them free of charge, with the exception of any charges incurred on behalf of members from third parties which are passed on at cost.

'The Railway' has never relied on gimmicks and is fiercely proud of the straightforward, easy-to-understand and competitive financial 'products' it offers whilst the Society's small dedicated staff enables it to offer a highly personal service.

Since its birth so long ago thousands of Stafford residents have benefited from an association with 'The Railway' having happily found the right track to home ownership.

Above: *New Banking Hall, opened 2002.*

Keeping count

The story of Stafford's Dean Statham accountancy firm is intimately connected with that of the Stafford Railway Building Society. The firm's partners have provided the Building Society with its Secretaries and Chief Executives from 1892 onwards.

The firm was founded in 1890 by George Dean who had previously been the chief internal auditor for the London and North Western Railway, as well as by then being a

Bottom: *Three generations of the Dean family, from left; George, Walter Senior and Walter.*

On Herbert Owen's retirement in 1953 Walter's son, Walter Richard Dean, who had been placed first in the whole country in the examinations of the Institute of Chartered Accountants in 1952, joined the firm.

Walter Richard Dean would be one of the practice's best known names, having become Mayor, Chief Magistrate and Leader of the Council before his death in 1996.

The name change to Dean Statham arrived in 1985. In 1972, what was then the firm of Dean & Son, had merged with Statham & Co, a well known North Staffordshire accountancy firm, with offices in Newcastle-under-Lyme, where the firm still has separate offices.

Director of the Stafford Railway Building Society: two years later he became the Society's Secretary.

At the outset the firm was based in St Mary's Grove where George Dean worked as an accountant, insurance agent and stockbroker.

When George Dean died suddenly in 1912 his son Walter took over the business at the age of just 21. Astonishingly Walter Dean would stay in practice for the next 60 years until his own death. In 1914 on the outbreak of the Great War Walter brought in a partner, Herbert Owen, and went off to join the fight, not returning to the firm until 1919.

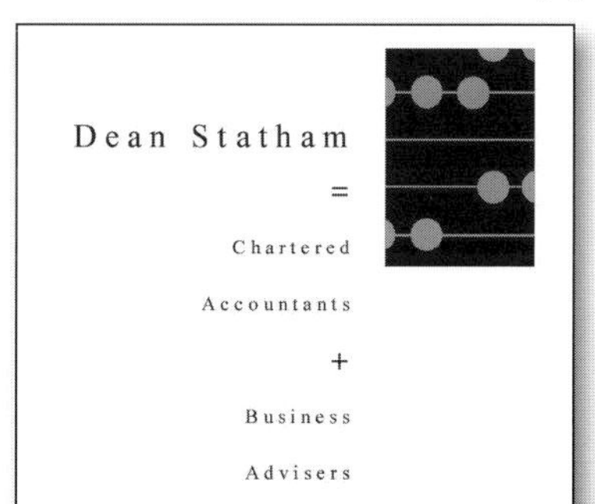

The practice had occupied its first premises for some 15 years before moving to premises in Market Square around 1905. The firm has occupied its present premises in Bank Passage off Market Square since 1927.

During the second world war Walter Dean senior was in charge of air raid precautions for Stafford, with the firm's office being in effect the air raid precautions headquarters for Stafford (fortunately upon which few bombs fell).

Today, though the long association with the Stafford Railway Building Society continues, Dean Statham remains, as it always has been, a major independent accountancy practice in its own right. You name it, and if it comes under the umbrella of accountancy, the firm can help. Whether it's a start up, a small or medium sized business, a long established company, a subsidiary of a European company, or a local farmer or individual looking for some sound independent financial advice the firm has the expertise they need.

Every client is allocated an experienced partner to meet their personal requirements: highly qualified specialists back up the partners, so combining experience with technical expertise in such areas as taxation, farming, insolvency, financial services to commerce industry and professions such as doctors and solicitors.

Top : *Present office in Bank Passage.*
Above: *Abacus: Logo of the firm.*

You make it, we'll take it

Lorries. You can't miss them as they pass up and down our motorways, carrying the lifeblood of industry and commerce along those great national arteries.

With increasing prosperity over the last thirty years more lorries than ever need to use our roads, and over those decades the names of some transport firm's have become increasingly familiar to regular motorway travellers.

Stan Robinson (Stafford) Ltd is one of those familiar names. The company is rapidly becoming one of the largest privately owned transport companies in the UK. It was founded in 1970 by Stan Robinson with one lorry which he drove himself.

Stan was born the second son of George and Bertha Robinson at Stowe by Chartley. George Robinson was the local coal merchant who worked out of Weston Station, and Stan started to work with his father at the very early age of seven. Unfortunately George had to give up the coal round when Stan was 14, but by then Stan had lorries in his blood and he was determined to one day have his own lorry.

But how to achieve that ambition? It wasn't going to be easy. Stan left school at 15 and went to work on farms. By the age of 18 however Stan got his first lorry-driving job at Armitage Shanks followed by a driving job with HW Hunt & Son and then at Richardson's of Rugeley. By this time however Stan had married his wife Florence 'Flo' and had three children, so at the age of 28 and needing better paid work, he left lorry driving to take a transport managers job; just six months later he was offered an even better paid job, but his boss asked instead 'Why don't you just buy your own lorry?'

After some deliberation Stan did exactly that. Taking a risk he bought his first lorry, and on 1st November 1970 Stan Robinson, owner-driver, started his own transport business from the bottom of his garden with that single second-hand vehicle.

In those days Stafford was a thriving town with GEC, Lotus, Euode Ltd, Universal and Dormans being the major employers. But there were already lots of local transport companies in Staffordshire: BRS, Nicholl's, WR Davies & Co Ltd, GM Plant & Son, Plant & Evans, Pickfords and

Top left: *Stan Robinson's vehicles taking part in the annual Truck Show at Peterborough.* ***Right:*** *This restored lorry is like one that Stan Robinson's father would have used on his coal round. This is now used at shows throughout the country.*

other companies such as Richardson's, Bassets and many others, including another new starter Ed Weetman. So who did this Stan Robinson think he was, and how was he going to make a living when faced with so much competition?

Stan started out by taking building blocks from Lignacite Ltd of Stafford up the M6 to building sites in Lancashire. He brought back cattle food for HW Hunt & Son Ltd, delivering to local farms; this was all loaded and unloaded by hand: there were no pallets and fork-lifts in those days.

Top: *Inside the main warehouse.*
Above and right: *Vehicle maintenance taking place on-site.*

Then in August 1971 came Stan's first new Ford articulated lorry, and with it three trailers. September 1971 saw the first driver employed. Now things really began to move. The years 1972-73 saw the fleet increase to six vehicles and Stan stopped driving in order to man the office. Work expanded, but not however into Stafford as in those days the town was in effect still a closed shop to newcomers. But there was a way to resolve even that problem.

August 1975 saw the acquisition of another company when Stan bought out WH Davis & Co Ltd. The eight lorries and one van which came with the purchase were more than welcome, but more importantly the firm also came with its customers - customers which included all the main factories in Stafford: this was the key to the future.

Not surprisingly more space was needed. In 1978 Stan moved the growing operation to its present depot and head office at Ladfordfields, Seighford, which was then a 2 1/2 acre site (but which now extends to 22 1/2 acres) and which is strategically positioned in the centre of the UK, and just three miles from the M6.

But even that would prove to be only a start. In 1985 Stan bought a Scottish company to

provide the firm with its first depot in Glasgow. The Scottish company's fleet of 18 lorries took Stan's total fleet to 50. Increasing range and a larger number of lorries now led to a change in company strategy: a move began away from 'full load' work, a move which would ultimately turn the company into a nation-wide distributor of goods on pallets.

Subsequently the company opened a depot at Willand in Devon. Stan had originally sent five lorries there to do the West Country deliveries and to try and find work to send back: today that depot operates 25 vehicles in the South West from a six acre site.

Later the company also bought another small business in Darlington and turned that into a North East depot. In 2001 Stan acquired a company in Ipswich to be his East Anglian depot. By 2002 the company had a fleet of 160 vehicles and employed 260 people.

How has this remarkable growth been achieved? Partly it has been down to sound business practices. From the outset Stan set out his basic business principles: 'we can do any job if the price is right, pay good money and employ good people, and treat people like you would like to be treated yourself'.

Following those precepts for more than 30 years the company has been grown by hard work and dedication from Stan, his family and all his employees. Long service is commonplace: two employees have completed 25 years with the company and half of the employees are into double figures in years of service. Stan is particularly proud that it has all been achieved without employing a salesperson at any time; in his words 'our service has been our best salesman'. Not surprisingly then that the company was voted Motor Transport Haulier of the Year in 1999.

Top: *Some of Stan Robinson's haulage fleet.* ***Above right:*** *Stan Robinson's 'Roadtrain'.* ***Left:*** *One of the firm's lorries.*

Today the company remains a family business with Stan Robinson as its Managing Director. The other Directors are Stan's wife Flo and their three children, Mark, Ian and Pauline who all take an active part in running the business. From its head office in Stafford the company's speciality is next day, and two to three day, delivery of pallet consignments across the whole United Kingdom: an urgent consignment can leave Cornwall one day and arrive in Scotland the next.

That standard of service is achieved through overnight travel with vehicles meeting at the central hub in Stafford where consignments are transferred and forwarded to the appropriate area depot for delivery next day.

The area depots, together with the Head Office, are all connected through a 'Road runner' computer system through which all goods in transit can be traced, whether on a vehicle or in any of the company's increasingly large warehouses which exist at every location and where a storage and picking service is available to customers both large and small.

Each depot has its own workshops for the continuous repair and maintenance of the vehicle fleet. There is even an axle weighbridge at each location to ensure that no lorry is ever overloaded .

The whole operation is run 24 hours a day from early Monday morning until noon on Saturdays. Office staff, warehouse personnel, drivers and workshop technicians work a shift system to ensure the continuity and efficient operation of the service. The company even has its own training school in Stafford to ensure that staff are adequately trained and achieve the qualifications necessary to do their jobs to the highest standards.

And what of the future? Though understandably proud of its past Stan Robinson (Stafford) Ltd is also a forward looking company; now heavily reliant on computers and IT it is always looking at ways to improve in the future. Stan for example is an active promoter of the Road Train concept: dual-trailer lorries which would reduce road congestion and travel overnight on designated, approved routes. The importance of continuing to grow has not been forgotten either, and the company intends to expand further by opening one or more new depots to maintain and improve the standard of service required by, and available to, customers whilst taking into account the present and future restrictions being imposed on the transport industry by the British government and the European Union.

Not a bad record for a firm which started out with just one second-hand lorry!

Top left: *An aerial view of the premises.*
Above right: *Another view of the 'Roadtrain' on trial.*
Below: *Staff during a visit to London where the firm received the 'Haulier of the Year' Award in 1999.*

Ed held high

Ed Weetman (Haulage & Storage) Ltd must be one of the few transport companies around which doesn't worry when we get a bad winter.

The prospect of a hard winter holds no horrors at all for this business, based at the Pasture Fields Enterprise Park because one of the company's ongoing contracts is delivering road salt for gritting throughout Staffordshire, Lincolnshire and East Anglia - the harder the weather the greater demand.

But distributing rock salt is only a fraction of the work undertaken by this specialist haulage firm started by Ed Weetman in 1967.

Ed Weetman was born into a farming family at Fradswell where his father, Thomas, kept dairy cattle. Ed however preferred to pursue an engineering career, and after attending a National Certificate course at Rodbaston he joined the Gascoigne milking machine company in 1959, before briefly returning to farming when his father became ill.

In the 1960s transport lured Ed away from farming and he bought an old Morris 1100 pick up truck, the first vehicle in what would one day grow into a whole fleet of lorries.

'One of my first jobs was unloading 100 tons of sugar beet pulp in sacks for use as animal feed from ten wagons off a train in sidings in Stafford' Ed recalled. 'I had just two days to do it, and worked single-handed, completing about a dozen journeys to finish the job'.

Those two days of hard labour also saw the start of a continuing relationship with the British Sugar Corporation. At the end of the 20th century Trident Feeds, part of BSC, would be Ed Weetman's biggest customer. By then Ed Weetman Ltd had become one of the largest sole owner operators of its type, specialising in the storage and distribution of animal feed all over the country.

The company operates 40 tipper and bulk blowing vehicles, most of then Volvos supplied through Hartshorne (Potteries), from its nine acre site on the main A51 at Great Haywood, and from four storage depots strategically located in the Midlands, the North west and the North.

'When I was unloading that train at Stafford I could not visualise that the company would grow as it has.' Ed reflected in 1997, the 30th anniversary of starting out, 'My first commercial vehicle was an old lorry bought from a scrapyard for £80. I had to borrow half the money from

Top left: *Ed Weetman.* ***Above right:*** *Ed Weetman and his wife, Gill.* ***Right:*** *Recent additions to the Weetman fleet.*

Mr Fred Watson of F Watson & Sons in Stone. I paid him back at £5 a week and will never forget how he helped me get started. My next vehicle was a second-hand Commer which cost me £400 and that, indirectly, saw the start of my association with Hartshorne because I met the father of John Goode who would one day become Hartshorne's Managing Director at Stoke.'

Ed Weetman began using second-hand Volvos in 1971 and the company bought its first new ones in 1977. In 1997 the company bought ten new Volvo articulated lorries from Hartshorne's in a single year.

Weetman's association with Hartshorne Trucks would be a very close one. Ed Weetman explained: 'We started off doing our own maintenance and service but today's sophisticated modern trucks are more than a hammer and a spanner job and lorries have to be maintained and serviced by specialist mechanics. So we rented our workshop to Hartshornes where they maintain all our vehicles and trailers in addition to the vehicles of other customers as well'.

Ed Weetman has maintained a site at Great Haywood since 1977 after originally buying a small transport café standing on about an acre of land. Today the company employs around 60 people in addition special sub-contractors who are called in to meet seasonal demand which peaks in excess of 20,000 tonnes a week.

At the start of the new millennium Ed Weetman and his wife had returned to their roots, running a 200 acre farm with 300 head of cattle; and Ed was now President of the Birmingham and District Agricultural Society - in addition to still keeping a close eye on the lorries which bear his name.

Top right: *Ed Weetman with one of the many successful race-horses that he has bred.* ***Left:*** *The firm's headquarters.* ***Below:*** *Two of the Ed Weetman fleet.*

A moving story

For those who enjoy the beauty, and indeed the occasional mystery, of the English language 'Pantechnicon' is a particularly attractive word. It's a word derived from the classical Greek language and literally means 'of many arts' though it, or rather 'pantekhnikon', was then the name of a bazaar or market. In Victorian England the original Pantechnicon was a department store in London, a building in which it was intended to sell all kinds of artistic work but which was eventually turned into a furniture store. That usage led in turn to the 'pantechnicon-van', a horse-drawn vehicle used to deliver furniture. Today pantechnicon is the name universally applied to all large removal vans. And a local removal firm which has been around for almost as long as pantechnicons is that of Horsleys of Stafford.

Top left: *An early press advertisement for the firm.* ***Right:*** *A removal vehicle in the 1950s.* ***Below:*** *Two horsepower transportation in the early 1900s.*

Some time before 1890 former railway worker Thomas Horsley and his sons Ernest and Walter decided to set themselves up as carters, delivering coal and arranging household removals.

The firm started life from 95 Marston Road in Stafford where the family trio would eventually be joined by Robert Horsley, Ernest' son, the next generation of the Horsley family. Little did they realise that by the dawn of the 21st century five generations of the family would have been involved in the business.

In the earliest days carts pulled by horses were the only vehicles available, though the firm would move on to using steam-powered vehicles before eventually settling on

today's ubiquitous internal combustion engine. But that was still far in the future. By the time Thomas Horsley came to retire, on a pension of 24 shillings (£1.20) a week, he was able to hand over only four horses, three carts and three coal drays to his sons.

Horsleys would stay based in Marston Road for an astonishing 50 years before moving to Stafford's Oxford Gardens, then later to Bellasis Street, Fancy Walk before finally moving to the firm's present headquarters in Marsh Street and its premises at Pasture-fields, Great Haywood.

The first move had taken place near the end of the second world war. The firm's removal work had been largely suspended for the duration of the war whilst Horsleys were awarded a contract to deliver coal to the RAF, helping the war effort by keeping our brave lads in the Airforce warm until it was time for them to take to the air and carry the war to the Hun from the skies.

After the war coal deliveries began a gradual decline; not least from the 1950s when repeated lethal smogs plagued our cities giving impetus to the call for cleaner air. The Clean Air Acts of that decade led to gas, electricity and oil becoming the domestic heating fuels of choice and the familiar sight of the coal man became ever rarer. In response, and with even less demand for coal likely in the future, Horsleys now concentrated more and more on the removals side of the business.

Today, with coal deliveries now part of the distant past, commercial, office and domestic relocations form the backbone of the business, with a direct road service to all European destinations and a packing and shipping service to any port or city in the world.

Horses and carts of course have gone the same way as coal deliveries. In the 21st century Horsleys use the most modern up to date equipment and vehicles, and offer their customers modern containerised storage facilities.

Though now able to boast more than a century of successful trading, and a file full of recommendations which go back to the reign of Queen Victoria, Horsleys still aims to remain a family business and continue to offer what it has done for so long already - providing a high class, reliable removal service, whilst still striving to expand the business.

The present head of the firm is Robert Horsley; with his sons Russell, Nigel and Joe now in partnership with him it looks as if the Horsley name is going to continue to be a familiar one in Stafford for many years still to come. And pantechnicons? Well, as you might expect, these days Horsleys has a whole fleet of them, all decked out in the firm's distinctive blue livery and ready to move anyone, anywhere at any time.

Above: *A removal vehicle from the 1960s.* ***Left and below:*** *Horsleys modern fleet of removal vehicles for the 21st century.*

Power from people

Stafford has a long association with the engineering industry; especially the building of diesel engines which provide the power to move everything from humble farm tractors to powerful ocean going ships. In the opening years of the 21st century the most important local firm is Perkins Engines Company Limited.

In 1932 F Perkins Ltd was founded by entrepreneurial businessman and engineer Frank Perkins. Operating from a tiny workshop in Peterborough the company employed just seven people, including Frank himself; the first diesel engine was produced after just a few months. The engine was the world's first high-speed diesel engine: Frank named it the Vixen.

That first engine evolved to become the Fox and later the Wolf - an engine that in the 1930s came to fame setting world speed records in racing cars and also took Frank to Moscow in a Hillman saloon car.

The first year's production was just 35 engines, all destined for trucks and cars; but throughout the next three decades production rocketed as a succession of engines were developed for agricultural and other off-highway uses - 1962 saw the millionth engine exported. With a wide range of products and multi-sector applications Perkins had by then turned high volume batch manufacturing into a fine art, such that by 1981 over five million engines had been built in Peterborough.

In 1994 Perkins bought Dorman Diesels Ltd and its Tixall Road Works in Stafford.

The history of Dorman Diesels went back to 1870 when William Henry Dorman founded a relatively modest enterprise in Foregate Street with the aim of producing specialist machine tools for the shoe industry. The Tixall

***Right:** An extension to the Foregate Street works, opened in 1913.* ***Below:** Dorman workers in the foundry of Tixall Works in the 1920s.*

Dorman name was still one to be reckoned with its engines featuring in power generators, huge dumper trucks, trawlers, cranes and excavators; it was a very attractive company.

In the 1980s Dorman engineers undertook a major review of engine technology with the design brief of creating an engine for the year 2000, the new SE engine range was developed using the very latest engineering techniques. New development and computerised testing facilities were installed as part of the programme and in 1984 Dorman launched the 6SE, the first of the SE Series of engines. In 1987 Broadcrown acquired Dorman Diesels before being purchased by Perkins Engines in 1994.

Now an independent subsidiary of the Caterpillar Group, Perkins has three manufacturing sites in the UK, and licensees around the world adding to the total, over fifteen million Perkins engines had been produced since its small beginning. Frank Perkins died in 1967 but, though ownership of the company may have changed several times, his vision and values live on through the people who continue to make Perkins Engines Company Limited the vital business it is today.

Top: *Current manufacturing at Perkins Stafford, 2002.*
Below: *Perkins Tixall Road site, 2002.*

Road site was acquired by WH Dorman & Co Ltd in 1925, by which time the once small business had already become a major engineering company employing 2,000 local craftsmen in its factory which had grown up next to WH Dorman's former home and original small workshop. There a vast range of machinery was produced: aero engines, petrol engines, gun parts, rock drills and die casting machines to name but a few. The first diesel engines were produced at Tixall Road in the 1930s. At the end of that decade the Foregate Street Works were occupied by the Ministry of Defence and would not be used by the company again until the 1970s. During the war years Tixall Road was turned over to meeting the demands of the war effort under the Admiralty, for which Dorman's would make a vast number of marine engines and generating sets.

The economic war which followed the end of the second world war lead to a massive increase in exports from Dorman. By 1952 more than 85 per cent of the company's output was going overseas with the company's engines appearing in major engineering projects throughout the world.

At the end of the 1950s Dorman's merged with one of its closest customers, WG Bagnall Ltd on the other side of Stafford, which had been using Dorman diesels in its railway locomotives for many years.

In 1961 the first of a series of further mergers took place when Dorman merged with the English Electric Group. Seven years later English Electric itself merged with GEC. But by the 1970s the

Set in stone

According to the history books the Stone Age ended more than three thousand years ago. But that's a lie. Stone, nature's most enduring building material, has never really gone out of favour. And that's hardly a surprise, if we want something to last we make it from granite or marble, not wood or iron.

Memorials are things we really want to last down the ages. The ancients knew that if a thing was to be seen by generations yet to come it had to be made of stone. Some of their creations have lasted an awful long time: the great Pyramids of Egypt and the even older Stonehenge, to pick but two.

These and many other antiquities are memorials not just to the kings and queens, emperors, empresses and pharaohs who ordered them to be built but equally, if unintentionally, to the immensely skilled craftsmen who worked on them. It's no wonder that the mason's compass and set square remain symbolic representations of knowledge and power to this day, and that skilled monumental masons are still respected and admired though hundreds of other trades have been shorn of their mystique under the twin hammer blows of mechanisation and automation.

In the 1980s The Old Lock Up building in Stafford town was refurbished. The building was where many years ago the town drunks once spent the night. A local firm of monumental masons, Benton's, did much of the restoration work.

It was a century earlier, in 1884, that stone mason George Jabez Benton, the son of the miller at Hammerwich, first set up his own business.

Benton's stone masonry and monumental workshop was run in those far off days from 98 Eccleshall Road - exactly the same address that the firm still operates from.

Top left: *Company founder George Jabez Benton.* ***Above right:*** *The plaque commemorating the soldiers who lost their lives at Gommercourt in 1916.* ***Below:*** *Far right is a modern headstone designed to be in keeping with older memorials.* ***Right:*** *County Buildings, Stafford where Benton's added the latest inscriptions and did the re-gilding of the existing inscriptions on the main staircase.*

George Benton's three sons Charles, George and Frederick would follow their father in the business. Under the founder's sons monumental mason's yards, all bearing the Benton name, would be subsequently set up in Eccleshall Road, Stafford and Burton-on-Trent.

The late 19th century and early 20th were a golden age for the monumental mason. Today superb examples of the stone mason's art can still be found in every cemetery in and around Stafford.

Astonishingly five generations of the Benton family would work in the business before the last Benton left to go into computing, leaving the firm to its present owners Nigel Robinson and Paul Mars, each with more than a quarter of a century in the trade behind him.

Masonry work for public and private clients continues to form the core of the firm's business. Gravestones, house names and other types of masonry work are all supplied to the general public, whilst more dramatic projects are undertaken for clients such as local authorities.
In the 1980s when a memorial plaque was required for the Falklands Memorial Garden on the Four Clocks Island

Benton's did all the work. In the same decade a carved plaque of north Staffordshire was sent to Gommecourt in France.

Paul Mars and Nigel Robinson have also worked on the Royal Artillery Memorial Garden and on re-gilding the main staircase in Stafford's County Buildings as well as its prison - Benton's having carved the plaque over the visitors' gate and centre.

Although, since the firm was founded in the reign of Queen Victoria, steam-driven cross cut saws may have been replaced by diamond saws and corers along with modern sand-blasting equipment, nevertheless hand tools are still used extensively. Hammers and chisels, allied with years of experience, can produce work that no machine could ever hope to match. When Staffordshire's First World War Memorial needed work on it, the Borough Council, responsible for the monument in Victoria Park, inevitably brought in Benton's as part of a special project to revamp the memorial. Nigel Robinson spent several days re-carving the worn names on the memorial by hand.

Whether any of Benton's work will still be around in another three thousand years for our descendants to admire is more than we dare speculate. What we can be sure of however is that today's fine craftsmanship in stone will easily see us out, ensuring that examples of Benton's millennia old skill in monumental masonry will continue to be seen for many generations to come.

Top left: *The firm's current partners Nigel Robinson and Paul Mars.* ***Top right:*** *Nigel Robinson re-carving the names on the Staffordshire War Memorial.*
Above left: *The Badge of the Royal Artillery.*
Below: *The Commemoration Stone in the Royal Artillery Memorial Garden at Alrewas in Staffordshire.*

Doing it 24 hours a day

One thing we all worry about is our car breaking down in some inhospitable spot. That's when we need a recovery vehicle to either get us back on the road or tow us to the nearest garage. And if we are lucky our saviour will be sent from Stafford.

Davies Motors was founded back in May 1965 by Eric Davies, armed with just seven pounds and ten shillings, a box of tools and a strong determination to succeed. In the early days Eric set the high standards which would endure into the 21st century. One day the firm would have a whole fleet of recovery vehicles; to begin with however Eric started out by buying a Land Rover with a crane attachment and operated from a small site at the rear of the Crown Inn on Lichfield Road.

In 1976 Yvonne Davies, Eric's eldest daughter, joined the business and it was decided to remodel the business as a Recovery Centre able to cope with all major breakdowns, repairs and accidents, concentrating on the light vehicle market. That year saw Davies Motors start working for most of the major breakdown organisations targeting the 'Get You Home' market.

This was a turning point for the business. Over the next few years new vehicles were acquired and extra land on the Lichfield Road site, which had been acquired in the 1980s, enabled the base to be upgraded.

The company's reputation would be made by never saying no. Through recession of the 1980s the company continued to grow. The recovery firm which had once been a one man operation now had 15 staff and 12 vehicles.

By the early years of the new century continuing expansion saw Eric's daughter Yvonne having become Operations Director whilst her younger sister Angie, who had joined the firm in 1988, was Administration and Car Rental Manager. The once tiny firm now had some 30 staff and 21 recovery vehicles, all operated from its increasingly busy Lichfield Road premises but spread all over the country, providing national coverage all day every day of the year - as the company motto cheerfully reminds motorists 'We do it 24 hours a day'!

Right: *One of the current fleet of vehicles.* ***Below:*** *The recovery fleet from the 1970s.*

The family fleet

The blue-liveried lorries of H Nickolls & Son (Milford) based at The Green in Milford are a familiar sight around Stafford. The firm was founded in 1923 by present managing director John Nickolls' grandfather, Hubert Nickolls. The 'son' in the firm's name refers to Hubert's son Brian Nickolls who retired in the late 1990s. In the early days the firm had it's own gravel quarry. The company also ran the local bus service until 1967.

During the second world war Nickolls also delivered coal as well as running a coach service. After the war the quarry was sold and the company switched to what it did best - road haulage and coach services. By then the fleet numbered some 20 vehicles.

Up until the 1970s most of the work was with tippers and block earth moving and the company was heavily involved in building the M6. In the 1970s however the firm diversified into waste disposal and skip hire

John Nickolls joined his father Brian in the business in 1988 after spending nine years in the Royal Navy swapping a fleet of ships for a fleet of lorries. After driving company vehicles for ten years John next swapped his cab seat for one behind the managing director's desk. David Nickolls joined his brother in 1991. Meanwhile some of the company's 20 employees have been with the firm for more than 25 years: fitter Arthur Worrall with four decades under his belt would see many changes in the vehicles passing through his hands, not least that modern cabs make engines far easier to access.

More than 50 years after the end of the war Nickolls is still running a fleet of exactly 20 lorries, though the type of vehicle has changed considerably over the years - and their cost: the company now buys only new vehicles and will spend up to £50,000 for the right lorry.

With a philosophy of offering a quality service to its existing and prospective customers the firm looks set to be constantly busy well into the 21st century and aims to expand steadily, thus ensuring that the Nickolls name remains a familiar one on the country's roads for some considerable time to come.

Top left: *Hubert Nickolls.* ***Above left:*** *A skip loader from the 1970s.* ***Left:*** *One of the firm's coaches from the 1960s.* ***Below:*** *One of the firm's current vehicles.*

Pupils at St Michael's School, Bagley line up to collect their Coronation Mugs in 1937.

Acknowledgments

The publishers would like to thank

Staffordshire Arts and Museum Service

Stafford Historical & Civic Society

Mr Chris Copp

Mr W J Read

Mr I Tavernor

Steve Ainsworth

True North Books Ltd - Book List

Memories of Accrington - 1 903204 05 4
Memories of Barnet - 1 903204 16 X
Memories of Barnsley - 1 900463 11 3
Golden Years of Barnsley -1 900463 87 3
Memories of Basingstoke - 1 903204 26 7
Memories of Bedford - 1 900463 83 0
More Memories of Bedford - 1 903204 33 X
Golden Years of Birmingham - 1 900463 04 0
Birmingham Memories - 1 903204 45 3
Memories of Blackburn - 1 900463 40 7
More Memories of Blackburn - 1 900463 96 2
Memories of Blackpool - 1 900463 21 0
Memories of Bolton - 1 900463 45 8
More Memories of Bolton - 1 900463 13 X
Bolton Memories - 1 903204 37 2
Memories of Bournemouth -1 900463 44 X
Memories of Bradford - 1 900463 00 8
More Memories of Bradford - 1 900463 16 4
More Memories of Bradford II - 1 900463 63 6
Bradford Memories - 1 903204 47 X
Bradford City Memories - 1 900463 57 1
Memories of Bristol - 1 900463 78 4
More Memories of Bristol - 1 903204 43 7
Memories of Bromley - 1 903204 21 6
Memories of Burnley - 1 900463 95 4
Golden Years of Burnley - 1 900463 67 9
Memories of Bury - 1 900463 90 3
Memories of Cambridge - 1 900463 88 1
Memories of Cardiff - 1 900463 14 8
Memories of Carlisle - 1 900463 38 5
Memories of Chelmsford - 1 903204 29 1
Memories of Cheltenham - 1 903204 17 8
Memories of Chester - 1 900463 46 6
More Memories of Chester -1 903204 02 X
Memories of Chesterfield -1 900463 61 X
More Memories of Chesterfield - 1 903204 28 3
Memories of Colchester - 1 900463 74 1
Nostalgic Coventry - 1 900463 58 X
Coventry Memories - 1 903204 38 0

Memories of Croydon - 1 900463 19 9
More Memories of Croydon - 1 903204 35 6
Golden Years of Darlington - 1 900463 72 5
Nostalgic Darlington - 1 900463 31 8
Darlington Memories - 1 903204 46 1
Memories of Derby - 1 900463 37 7
More Memories of Derby - 1 903204 20 8
Memories of Dewsbury & Batley - 1 900463 80 6
Memories of Doncaster - 1 900463 36 9
Nostalgic Dudley - 1 900463 03 2
Golden Years of Dudley - 1 903204 60 7
Memories of Edinburgh - 1 900463 33 4
Memories of Enfield - 1 903204 14 3
Memories of Exeter - 1 900463 94 6
Memories of Glasgow - 1 900463 68 7
More Memories of Glasgow - 1 903204 44 5
Memories of Gloucester - 1 903204 04 6
Memories of Grimsby - 1 900463 97 0
More Memories of Grimsby - 1 903204 36 4
Memories of Guildford - 1 903204 22 4
Memories of Halifax - 1 900463 05 9
More Memories of Halifax - 1 900463 06 7
Golden Years of Halifax - 1 900463 62 8
Nostalgic Halifax - 1 903204 30 5
Memories of Harrogate - 1 903204 01 1
Memories of Hartlepool - 1 900463 42 3
Memories of High Wycombe - 1 900463 84 9
Memories of Huddersfield - 1 900463 15 6
More Memories of Huddersfield - 1 900463 26 1
Golden Years of Huddersfield - 1 900463 77 6
Nostalgic Huddersfield - 1 903204 19 4
Huddersfield Town FC - 1 900463 51 2
Memories of Hull - 1 900463 86 5
More Memories of Hull - 1 903204 06 2
Memories of Ipswich - 1 900463 09 1
More Memories of Ipswich - 1 903204 52 6
Memories of Keighley - 1 900463 01 6
Golden Years of Keighley - 1 900463 92 X
Memories of Kingston - 1 903204 24 0

Available in the Local Interest section of all major bookshops or direct from the publishers - telephone 01422 344344

True North Books Ltd - Book List

Memories of Leeds - 1 900463 75 X
More Memories of Leeds - 1 900463 12 1
Golden Years of Leeds - 1 903204 07 0
Memories of Leicester - 1 900463 08 3
More Memories of Leicester - 1 903204 08 9
Memories of Leigh - 1 903204 27 5
Memories of Lincoln - 1 900463 43 1
Memories of Liverpool - 1 900463 07 5
More Memories of Liverpool - 1 903204 09 7
Liverpool Memories - 1 903204 53 4
Memories of Luton - 1 900463 93 8
Memories of Macclesfield - 1 900463 28 8
Memories of Manchester - 1 900463 27 X
More Memories of Manchester - 1 903204 03 8
Manchester Memories - 1 903204 54 2
Memories of Middlesbrough - 1 900463 56 3
More Memories of Middlesbrough - 1 903204 42 9
Memories of Newbury - 1 900463 79 2
Memories of Newcastle - 1 900463 81 4
More Memories of Newcastle - 1 903204 10 0
Memories of Newport - 1 900463 59 8
Memories of Northampton - 1 900463 48 2
More Memories of Northampton - 1 903204 34 8
Memories of Norwich - 1 900463 73 3
Memories of Nottingham - 1 900463 91 1
More Memories of Nottingham - 1 903204 11 9
Nottingham Memories - 1 903204 63 1
Bygone Oldham - 1 900463 25 3
Memories of Oldham - 1 900463 76 8
Memories of Oxford - 1 900463 54 7
Memories of Peterborough - 1 900463 98 9
Golden Years of Poole - 1 900463 69 5
Memories of Portsmouth - 1 900463 39 3
More Memories of Portsmouth - 1 903204 51 8
Nostalgic Preston - 1 900463 50 4
More Memories of Preston - 1 900463 17 2
Preston Memories - 1 903204 41 0
Memories of Reading - 1 900463 49 0
Memories of Rochdale - 1 900463 60 1
More Memories of Reading - 1 903204 39 9
More Memories of Rochdale - 1 900463 22 9
Memories of Romford - 1 903204 40 2
Memories of St Albans - 1 903204 23 2
Memories of St Helens - 1 900463 52 0
Memories of Sheffield - 1 900463 20 2
More Memories of Sheffield - 1 900463 32 6
Golden Years of Sheffield - 1 903204 13 5
Memories of Slough - 1 900 463 29 6
Golden Years of Solihull - 1 903204 55 0
Memories of Southampton - 1 900463 34 2
More Memories of Southampton - 1 903204 49 6
Nostalgic Stafford - 1 903204 64 X
Memories of Stockport - 1 900463 55 5
More Memories of Stockport - 1 903204 18 6
Memories of Stockton - 1 900463 41 5
Memories of Stoke-on-Trent - 1 900463 47 4
More Memories of Stoke-on-Trent - 1 903204 12 7
Memories of Stourbridge - 1903204 31 3
Memories of Sunderland - 1 900463 71 7
More Memories of Sunderland - 1 903204 48 8
Memories of Swindon - 1 903204 00 3
Memories of Uxbridge - 1 900463 64 4
Memories of Wakefield - 1 900463 65 2
More Memories of Wakefield - 1 900463 89 X
Nostalgic Walsall - 1 900463 18 0
Golden Years of Walsall - 1 903204 56 9
More Memories of Warrington - 1 900463 02 4
Memories of Watford - 1 900463 24 5
Golden Years of West Bromwich - 1 900463 99 7
Memories of Wigan - 1 900463 85 7
Golden Years of Wigan - 1 900463 82 2
Nostalgic Wirral - 1 903204 15 1
Memories of Woking - 1 903204 32 1
Nostalgic Wolverhampton - 1 900463 53 9
Wolverhampton Memories - 1 903204 50 X
Memories of Worcester - 1 903204 25 9
Memories of Wrexham - 1 900463 23 7
Memories of York - 1 900463 66 0